KU-696-229

CONTENTS

Acknowledgements

Aardman Animations Limited for the use of the film poster for *Chicken Run* entitled 'This ain't no chicken flick' © 2000, DreamWorks, Pathe and Aardman.

Wendy Cope for the use of material used in the marketing of *Making cocoa for Kingsley Amis* by Wendy Cope © 1985, Wendy Cope (1985, Faber and Faber).

Mary Dawson for the use of 'Freedom' by Mary Dawson from *This poem doesn't rhyme* edited by Gerard Benson © 1990, Mary Dawson (1990, Viking).

Eric Finney for the use of 'Haiku' by Eric Finney in *This Poem Doesn't Rhyme* edited by Gerard Benson © 1990, Eric Finney (1990, Viking).

David Higham Associates for the use of an extract from *The Snow Maze* by Jan Marks © 1992, Jan Marks (1992, Walker Books).

Christopher Little Literary Agency for the use of an extract from *Harry Potter and the Philosopher's Stone* by JK Rowling © 1997, JK Rowling (1997, Bloomsbury).

Marks and Spencer plc for the use of an extract from an advertisement for peaches which appeared in *Guardian Weekend* of 29 July 2000 © 2000, Marks and Spencer plc.

Mirror Group Newspapers Ltd for the use of the front page including the article "Lucky Lad" from *The Mirror* of 20 April 1999 © 1999, MGN Ltd (1999, MGN Ltd).

Tony Mitton for the use of a verse from 'Write-a-Rap Rap' by Tony Mitton from *The Moonlit Stream and other poems* edited by John Foster © 2000, Tony Mitton.

Penguin Books Ltd for the use of two extracts from *Something Else* by Kathryn Cave © 1994, Kathryn Cave (1994, Viking) and for the use of an extract from 'Each, Peach, Pear, Plum' from *Each, Peach, Pear, Plum* by Janet and Allan Ahlberg © 1978, Janet and Allan Ahlberg (1978, Penguin).

The Peters Fraser and Dunlop Group Ltd for the use of 'Down Behind the Dustbin' from *Wouldn't you like to know* by Michael Rosen © 1977, Michael Rosen (1977, Andre Deutsch); for the use of 8 lines from 'Poetry Jump Up' by James Berry from *Poetry Jump Up* complied by Grace Nichols © 1990, James Berry (1990, Puffin) and for the use of 15 words from 'The Babysitter' from *The Hypnotiser* by Michael Rosen © Michael Rosen (Andre Deutsch).

The Press Association for the use of an X-ray photograph from the front-page article "Lucky Lad" which appeared in *The Mirror* of 20 April 1999 © 1999, The Press Association (1999, Mirror Group Newspapers).

M & C Saatchi for permission to reproduce a British Airways advertisement.

The Society of Authors as the representatives of The Literary Trustees of Walter de la Mare for the use of part of 'The Listeners' from *The Complete Poems of Walter de la Mare* by Walter de la Mare © 1969, Walter de la Mare.

Transworld Publishers Ltd for the use of an extract from *Clockwork* by Philip Pullman © 1996, Philip Pullman (1996, Doubleday).

Walker Books Ltd for the use of an extract from *The Hidden House* by Martin Waddell © 1990, Martin Waddell (1990, Walker Books).

AP Watt Ltd. on behalf of Michael B Yeats for the use of extracts from 'He wishes for the cloths of heaven' from *The Collected Poems of WB Yeats Vol 1: The Poems* by WB Yeats © 1983, WB Yeats.

Every effort has been made to trace copyright holders and the publishers apologise for any omissions.

Understanding texts
Introduction

The tale of two driving instructors

"I could teach a monkey to drive given long enough".

These words, spoken by one of my driving instructors as he crumpled in despair, were my first encounter with the fact that I might clunk gears, slam breaks too hard and ride up over pavements forever.

He gave up.

I gave up.

Ten years later I decided to give it one last try. I sailed through a quick set of lessons and passed first time.

The difference lay with the instructor.

That final instructor held a vital key to teaching driving – he opened the bonnet.

When I ground the gears, he explained how gears mesh. When I broke so hard we kissed the dashboard, he explained what break fluid did. After I reversed onto the pavement, he drew a little diagram showing how steering made the wheels move.

I regularly come back to the two driving instructors when encountering teachers who struggle with aspects of literacy, who ask me how to engage children with reading or boost children's writing. That second instructor provided me with a subject knowledge about the car, such that I learned how to drive it.

Subject knowledge

In recent years the emphasis from groups like the Teacher Training Agency and the National Literacy Project have set aspirational levels of teacher subject knowledge to underpin the teaching of literacy. The necessity of good subject knowledge cannot be over emphasised. Inspection findings demonstrate it to be the bedrock of good teaching. Lack of it can be the rotten core of many poor lessons.

When it comes to working with texts, many teachers soon realise they are starting the development of subject knowledge on a different footing from those who start a similar pursuit in science, ICT or even grammar. Whereas many teachers are not sure if they know the detail behind refraction or erosion and may be unsure what a modal verb is, there is an instinctive feeling that we know enough about texts. Teachers, like all adults, grew up surrounded by texts. Most progressed through life reading and writing. They may never have split an atom or even care when they split an infinitive but they feel comfortable with books in chapters, newspapers reporting events and letters that complain.

Comfortable is fine – but it can lead to a complacency that lacks the right degree of reflection and rigour.

Watch two teachers sharing a story with a class. One will read it, ask for some thoughts, point something out in the picture. Another may deploy a fuller degree of subject knowledge and know exactly what they want children to learn from encounter with the text. This teacher will focus on an aspect, such as character. Such a teacher will know what traits children should gather about a character. They will know the way those traits are developed in the story and their questioning may focus on this. They will know some ways in which one character can be compared with another. They know the recipe behind the making of such texts and possess the critical faculties to guide the interpretation of the story.

This book presents a basic grounding in such subject knowledge.

Chapter 1 explores the structures of stories, looking at how events, characters and settings are developed in such

texts. This chapter is complemented by Chapter 2 which examines the range of fiction texts, looking at the breadth of stories and authors that should feature in text teaching.

Chapters 3 and 4 look at the reading and writing of non-fiction texts. Chapter 3 focuses on information retrieval, including strategies such as skimming and scanning, and examines the process of comprehension; Chapter 4 presents strategies for structuring the writing of a full range of non fiction texts. Taking specific types of text, such as reports and explanations, this chapter presents the sorts of information about structure and language features that will improve writing.

Chapter 5 draws on a wide range of poetry to illustrate the various features of poems, such as their metrical structure and language features.

Chapter 6 deals with texts used in performance such as playscripts and jokes.

Chapter 7 touches upon media texts, including newspapers and advertising – two vital examples of texts many readers think they know well. However a clearer understanding of the various features of these texts and how newspapers and adverts are constructed can resource the teaching of media texts.

What are texts?
The word 'text' is one of those fuzzily edged words. When you try to define it you discover it is not quite as simple as you first thought.

The National Literacy Strategy Framework for Teaching defines a text as 'language organised to communicate. Includes written, spoken and electronic forms'. This sound definition opens up the full possibilities of the word text: text involves features of communicative meanings and the way they interact. It is derived from the Latin word 'texere', (to weave), the same root for the word 'textile'. The image this conjures up can be useful because there is something about a text that weaves together language in an act of communication. Threads are woven into a whole and different ways of weaving produce different textiles. Taken together, the two definitions provide a technical and imaginative working definition of text with which to proceed.

Why subject knowledge?
At this stage it is worth reflecting why subject knowledge is such a vital part of good teaching, if only to convince anyone who has read this far that they need the rest of the book.

● **Subject knowledge structures the subject.** Subject knowledge provides the language with which to talk and think about the subject. This language about language can be shared with children but, most vitally, provides a list of ideas that can be drawn upon to structure good teaching in this area. Obviously there's more to good teaching of a subject than just knowing its name, but a definition is a necessary starting point. The surgeon knows more about the heart than just the name of the organ but we would all be disconcerted being operated on by someone who says 'I'm going to operate on your... what d'ya call it? ...pumpy thing inside you'. You can know more about a subject than its terminology but that does not make knowledge of such terminology irrelevant.

In practical terms, after reading a chapter on non-fiction writing the aim is that the reader should have a list of texts to hand that will form the basis of a sound range of texts for their curriculum.

● **Subject knowledge improves lessons.** Subject knowledge breaks into a slightly stodgy curriculum. In too many cases, the teaching of English has ground to a bit of a halt amongst children. They just tread water, practising the skills with which the teacher feels comfortable. It reminds me of the child who responded to a researcher's enquiry as to why he was learning to read with the response 'So I can stop'. A teacher with a good grasp of subject knowledge is like a navigator who can point out where to go next, who knows what lies ahead and who can give good directions.

But, as anyone who visits the British Museum regularly will tell you, subject knowledge can be a bummer! It's the classics teachers that spoil it. There they are, strolling round with their ten pupils in tow, never content to quietly point out and comment. They have to propound their great grasp of Tiglath-Pileser and his statue to the whole gallery, booming away through the stillness.

Subject knowledge comes with a health warning. It is only as good as the teacher's ability to use it sensitively. A quick comment that such and such a text '...is a sonnet, okay?' is not okay. To be used properly, the teacher's subject knowledge must be like the hand that holds the bicycle after the stabilisers have been removed – there to support while needed.

Good subject knowledge underpins good teaching. It isn't the same as good teaching. Good teaching involves allowing that secure grasp of the subject to be communicated carefully, revisited and modelled in a range of ways until the children have got it. That is why each aspect of subject knowledge in this book is supported by ideas for teaching.

● **Subject knowledge resources the teacher.** A grounding in subject knowledge resources the questioning and discussion of texts and the comparing of one with another. When asking children to think about the differences between one poem and another, it isn't enough just to show the two texts and leave it there. Subject knowledge is the additional axis to this task that structures how the comparison will be made, asking children to compare the sound system, the imagery and the metre between two poems.

One thing you realise watching subject enthusiasts is that a deeper grasp of the subject liberates the teacher from dependence on other people's ideas. It's the science teacher who really understands how planes fly who can devise various ways of showing the learner the principles involved in the process. The history teacher who knows the period he or she is teaching generates ideas, discussion points and questions without relying on a set of lesson notes cribbed from some resource book or other. Likewise in English, knowledge of the subject can take the teacher beyond the stage of just being 'kitted out' with ideas for classroom activities. It can develop the teacher's ability at devising their own material to communicate their own understanding of the subject.

On a practical note, this makes the aim of this book quite specific. While stories might be recommended and examples of news stories used, the aim of the book is to leave teachers equipped to find their own texts and not be reliant on the ones listed here. For this reason it is worth encouraging the reader from the outset to keep a good collection of references to texts that prove useful and inspiring as well as maintaining an actual collection of texts. A chocolate bar wrapper with interesting persuasive writing should serve as a model more than the one time it works. A newspaper cutting that works well should be kept and used again. My caretaker Arthur once gave me a cutting about a fisherman swallowed whole by a huge python, complete with bulging reptile photograph. It was the basis for years of lessons thereafter and proved a hit every time.

● **Subject knowledge makes teachers adventurous.**
Subject knowledge provides the security from which to be adventurous. The secure teacher will venture beyond the bog book or the reading scheme and draw in interesting new material.

The full potential of this little word 'text' is seen if we look at the wide variety of examples of 'language organised to communicate'. The field, of course, includes the Big Book, the little book and so on. It also embraces poster hoardings, jokes, soap operas, advertising jingles, video trailers, chocolate bar wrappers, pop videos – these are all examples of language woven together into a text. If teachers can creatively read such texts, maintaining a focus on clear learning objectives, then this approach opens a vast array of resources available to us.

Try it out and try it with a few texts. You could start with:
– song lyrics to a current Top 10 song
– documentary material from the local museum service
– your school's old log book
– a trip letter
– a column from the dictionary
– the full page advert in a telephone directory
– junk mail
– leaflets nabbed off a shop counter
– letters to the local paper
– a notice from the parents' notice board
– an advertising hoarding near your school
– a holiday brochure
– a page from the maths scheme
– a story in *The Beano*
– a day's page in the television guide
– a chocolate bar wrapper
– an urban myth
– none of the above – instead, use a text you have found!

If you don't know what to do with these now – in seven chapters you will.

Chapter 1

Understanding stories

Llist any three stories and ask yourself: what have these stories got in common? Despite the fact that individual stories differ greatly, there are some clear, common features that structure various narratives. These common elements of stories can be placed under broad headings that can greatly support the teacher in working with narrative texts.

Storylines

A storyline is a series of events linked together to form a story. To create the storyline, one event is developed into another. For a line such as 'I went to my friend's house' to develop into a storyline, it is essential that there is a second event, possibly followed by a third, fourth and so on. If it is to become a storyline then the visit to the friend's house needs, at the very least, a 'She was not at home' or 'She came to the door dressed as an alien'. In a story like that of Cinderella, a series of events follow one another as the story unfolds.

Subject facts

Significance of events
The various events within the storyline can differ in significance. In *The Snow-Walker's Son*, by Catherine Fisher, two characters stay at a desolate castle waiting to meet with the creature of the title. As they wait, they eat, go

for a walk, explore corridors and do a number of other things. These actions serve to build up the suspense of these chapters but are not particularly crucial to the story. The storyline would not be disrupted if they were removed. However, if the eventual meeting with the Snow Walker's son was removed, the whole of the second half of the story would be disrupted. To take another example, as she waits for her Fairy Godmother, Cinderella may weep, sweep or just gaze into the fire. These events will communicate her mood but none are as significant as that moment when the Fairy Godmother transforms her in readiness for the ball.

Connections
The progress of a storyline from event to event is maintained by language that signals the passage of time. This may vary from 'and... and... and... ' to 'Then... Later... Afterwards.... Three days later... ' Stories will vary in the amount of time they cover – *ZinderZunder,* by Philip Ridley, takes place over 24 hours, whilst each book in the 'Harry Potter' series takes place over a school year – and the ways in which chunks of time are presented.

Narrative order
The progress of events in a story do not necessarily follow a chronological order. At the end of 'The Frog Prince' the kissed and transformed prince tells how he came to be enslaved in the body of a frog. This event took place before the opening of the story. In *Krindlekrax,* by Philip Ridley, the action takes place over a few days within a London street. However, within those few days, events are recounted that took place years before the opening chapter of the story. Such flashbacks will often provide information that contributes to the main storyline, as when Ruskin, the hero of the story, is told of events that took place around the time when he was born. Alongside the reader, Ruskin realises how these events explain the presence of Krindlekrax, the monster living underneath his street.

Plot
The events of a storyline are like pearls. Like loose pearls, they could follow in a time sequence without being connected in any way – a pattern that is possibly present in a story like *Alice in Wonderland,* by Lewis Carroll, or in *Under Milk Wood,* by Dylan Thomas. However, it is more usual for such events to be connected, like pearls on a string. The connecting thread is the plot, an essential element of most storylines.

EM Forster suggested it was possible to distinguish between a basic story and a plot, presenting an example of the distinction:

'The King died and then the Queen died' is a story. 'The King died and then the Queen died of grief' is a plot.

This link between events, such that the King's death causes the Queen's death, is an example of a plot. Cause and effect link the events of a story in an unfolding plot.

Prediction

Prediction is an act the reader engages in when anticipating how a plot may develop. The reader might ask at each new development in the story: what caused the event and where is it leading the story? To extend Forster's example, on hearing that the King died there are any number of possible results of this plot. The Queen could rejoice or marry the knave! If, however, the story continues with the Queen becoming distraught and taking to her bed then the possibilities get narrower. As a reader reads further into a story, the possible outcomes of an event are narrowed into the course the story actually takes. The reader sets out with a range of predictions, stemming from the opening of the story. Reading involves seeing these possibilities narrowed down – and waiting to find out how this narrowing will work.

The opening

The opening of possibilities is particularly significant as a story opens. The opening pages of a story set the scene and engage the reader's interest, for example *Charlotte's Web*, by EB White, opens:

'Where's Papa going with that axe?' said Fern.

● An understanding of the way in which stories are structured is useful when teaching narrative reading and writing. Children need to be able to perceive the order in which events unfold in a story. An understanding of the main elements of stories will enable the teacher to explain features of stories such as any departure from the chronological order of events. Such an understanding will also equip the teacher's exploration of how writers can structure stories.

Why you need to know these facts

● Events are crucial in a child's comprehension of a

storyline. When sharing stories with the class, the children need to maintain an awareness of the significant events that are being threaded together to create the plot. Questioning and discussion around these key events are of particular importance in the early years and, throughout the primary age range, children need the opportunity to recount stories they have read or been told in their own words.

● Throughout the primary age range, children develop their story planning skills. An understanding of the linear way in which stories are plotted can inform this planning. Children need to be encouraged to link the events in their stories with increasing sophistication. They will move from writing simple, one sentence records of events, such as 'I went to the park' towards joining one event onto another, such as 'I went to the park and then I went to the shop'. As they begin to plan out stories with varied characters and settings they also need to link events in interesting ways. They need to import an element of plotting, with one event causing another.

● The way in which the various events of a narrative are plotted together can provide a useful focus for discussing these events. For any one event in a story there is the potential to ask (a) what caused this? (b) where will this lead? To answer the first question children can trace back the way in which one event led to another earlier in the story. The answer to the second question will obviously vary depending on whether children are already familiar with the whole story. If, for example, they have read the entire story of *Farmer Duck*, by Martin Waddell, and are asked these two questions about the meeting of the animals, their answers will demonstrate their perception of how the meeting led to the outcome of the story.

● There comes a point in the development of reading at which many children stop. They give up on the task. This often happens when children have learned the actual skills of reading and are about to progress from books they read in one sitting to more extended shorter novels. Indeed, one of the children interviewed as part of the Southgate Report on extending reading explained that he wanted to learn how to read 'so that he could stop it' (Southgate, Arnold and Johnson, 1981).

In my experience this flagging of enthusiasm for reading can be prevented if children are encouraged to anticipate the way in which events can unfold in a longer story, seeing the possibilities that open at the start of the story and hazarding predictions as to how things might progress. As their awareness of how the links between what they are reading now and what they will encounter next time they read develop, children maintain an interest in the longer books they might otherwise have put aside.

Vocabulary

Causality – the effect of one thing causing another.
Chronological order – the order in which events occur in time.
Flashbacks – a point at which a story 'flashes back' to events that took place earlier.
Plot – that which connects the events in a story, with one event causing another.
Prediction – anticipation of what might take place at a later stage in a story.
Storylines – a series of events organised into a story.

Amazing facts

As anyone who has seen the film *Casablanca* knows, the story hinges on whether Ilsa, played by Ingrid Bergman, will eventually leave Casablanca with her husband, played by Paul Heinried, or with Humphrey Bogart. However, throughout the filming of *Casablanca* the ending had not been decided and Ingrid Bergman herself didn't know which man she would end up with. The confusion on her face isn't all acting!

Common misconceptions

Suspense is not the same as surprise.
Looking at how events unfold and the expectations of audiences in films the great storyteller and director Alfred Hitchcock explained suspense in this way:

> *Suppose that there is a bomb underneath this table between us... There is an explosion. The public is* **surprised**... *Now, let us take a* **suspense** *situation. The bomb is underneath the table and the public* **knows** *it... The public* **is aware** *that the bomb is going to explode at one o'clock and there is a clock in the decor. The public can see that it is a quarter to one... The audience is longing to warn the characters on the screen... In the first case we have given the public fifteen seconds of* **surprise** *at the moment of the explosion. In the second case we have provided them with fifteen minutes of* **suspense**.
> (Quoted in *Hitchcock*, by F Truffaut)

Understanding stories

Teaching ideas

● Create a set of cards where each card shows one event from a story, for example 'Cinderella loses her slipper'. Jumble up the cards and ask the children to put them back in order. They can be set out in order on a table, pegged onto a line or put up on a wall. This activity can be developed in a number of ways:

– Children can look for the links between the events they are sequencing, seeing examples of how one of the events lead to another.

– Groups of children can each have a card on which they recount an event from a story. The group can then sequence one another's cards.

– Two sets of cards consisting of two sets of events from stories known to the children can be mixed together. They then have to discern one set of events from another and reorder the stories. Having sequenced a set of card, children can try thinking of extra cards for events that are missing, then write and slot these into place.

● Storylines can be represented diagramatically. This can involve drawing a line to represent the course of a story and charting events along the line using symbols or labels. Older children can vary this, having parallel lines for parallel plots or allowing the line to take a shape that shows something about the story. One example of this is the child whose diagram of *The Lion King* took a course out across the paper and back to the start, a route the symbolised the journey taken by the central character (see below).

As they map out various stories, the children will produce sets of charts that they can use as a good tool for comparing a range of stories. From these charts they can see the various ways in which stories open, events build up, the different sorts of events that occur in the middle of stories and the way endings round off the process.

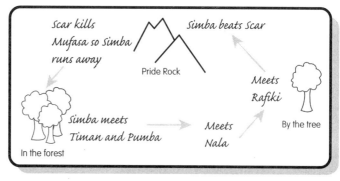

• Having read a range of intriguing story openings, ask the children to try devising their own interesting opening line or paragraph. This activity is sometimes best done if children are assured that having written the opening they do not need to write the rest of the story. They can then concentrate on the language and atmosphere of an opening to hook the reader. For example:

'That looks interesting,' Tariq said.

'Look out!' Mum shouted.

• Having begun a story as a class, ask the children to speculate about the possible outcomes, each writing their suggested outcome on a Post-It Note. These can be stuck on a chart at the front of the class for review as the story progresses. An extension of this activity is to divide the chart into sections labelled 'Likely', 'Even chance' and 'Unlikely'. The class can consider each Post-It possibility and vote on which space it should go in.

• Planning of stories can involve the reversal of the above activities. Ask the children to plan out a set of events that will take place, draw a diagram of how their story will progress, experiment with interesting openings and look at the range of possible events that could follow. Here, again, the use of various ways of planning stories is important. Children can work backwards from an ending or outwards from the middle of a story.

Characters

Readers of stories are often carried along by the events that take place, but it is often the characters that prove to be the most memorable aspects of a narrative. Personalities like Sherlock Holmes, Puck, Anancy and Mr Micawber all have the capacity to take root in the reader's memory.

Subject facts

Traits
The features of a character are known as his or her character traits. As readers we perceive certain qualities and build up certain opinions about a character. These are not usually the result of one event. The knowledge that a character is wicked does not come to the reader in the same way as the knowledge that they cast a spell on a princess. One is an event fixed at some point in the story. The other is

an impression that stands alongside the events, though may be formed as a result of a number of them.

Characterisation

Characterisation is the process by which a story builds up a picture of a character. It can take the form of direct characterisation, as when a story contains a direct statement about a character. For example, in *James and the Giant Peach,* by Roald Dahl, the two Aunts are introduced as 'Both really horrible people'. Such straightforward labelling of a character is particularly common in fairy stories and traditional tales with examples such as a 'crafty fox' or a 'kind fairy'.

Indirect characterisation is the more common form of characterisation in literature. Various aspects of a story indirectly contribute to the reader's perception of a particular character, such as:

● **Actions.** The things a character does contribute to their characterisation. In action films there is a common tendency to have the villain perform a particularly hideous action early in the film, turning the viewer against this villain. In *The Wolves Of Willoughby Chase,* by Joan Aiken, the collected actions of Miss Slighcarp, the wicked governess, lead the reader to see her for the villain she is. It isn't just the repeated actions of a character that build up the reader's impression. One-off actions, such as Willy's saving of Milly in *Willy the Wimp,* by Anthony Browne, can add to the complex picture.

● **Speech.** The speech or thoughts of a character add to the image they project. Willy's refrain of 'Oh, I'm sorry' in *Willy the Wimp* or the Farmer's hectoring 'How goes the work?' in *Farmer Duck* are examples of this.

● **Appearance.** In picture books, the look of a character can be particularly effective. For example the Wild Things in *Where the Wild Things Are,* by Maurice Sendak, make memorable pictures. Equally, the description of a character's appearance can prove evocative. Take, for example, the description of Hagrid in *Harry Potter and the Philosopher's Stone*, by JK Rowling:

> *His face was almost completely hidden by a long, shaggy mane of hair and a wild, tangled beard, but you could make out his eyes, glinting like black beetles under all the hair.*

- **Setting.** The places in which a character is encountered add to the overall impression. The character of Something Else, in Kathryn Cave's book *Something Else* is introduced with the sentence:

> *On a windy hill*
> *alone*
> *with nothing to be friends with*
> *lived Something Else.*

The lonely and windy hill are as much a reflection on the character of Something Else as the magical chocolate factory is on the character of Willy Wonka in *Charlie and the Chocolate Factory,* by Roald Dahl.

- **Analogy.** The appearance of one character with another can influence the reader's opinion of that character. There can be a contrast between characters in their actions and attitudes, so the reader's perception of Charlie Bucket in *Charlie and the Chocolate Factory* will in part be shaped by an impression of the other four children who behave so differently on the factory tour. This is used to full effect by Anthony Browne in *Voices in the Park* in which the same visit to a park is recounted by four different and contrasting characters, two parents and two children. The tendency to draw conclusions from comparisons between these diverse pairings is irresistible.

- **Names.** The names of characters can give some clue to what the reader can expect. Names can be as descriptive as Something Else or just conjure up an image, as with JK Rowling's friendly giant Hagrid.

Roles
The roles characters perform may vary. The basic difference between goodies and baddies, if somewhat simplistic, is still a vital part of the conflict that propels a story along. Some of the most common roles to be encountered in stories can be described as:

- **Heroine or hero.** This is often the central character who is solving a problem or finding something out.

- **Sender.** Sometimes the hero or heroine has been sent by another character, whether it be the gods or 'M'. This character sets the heroine/hero up with the task to be undertaken.

● **Helper.** The heroine, hero or villain will often be supported by a sidekick or helped along the way by other characters.

● **Villain.** Whatever the quest the above characters are hatching they will often be opposed by a villain. Sometimes the capture or frustration of the villain is the very task in which they are involved.

There will not be a character to neatly fit each role in every story, but within many children's stories it is possible to see characters who fulfil some, or all, of these roles.

They are particularly evident in traditional tales such as myths and fairy tales (see pages 48–9). Most have a heroine or hero and a villain. Many heroines and heros have a helper and are sent by another character. For example:

	Kate Crackernuts	Perseus and the Gorgon
Hero/Heroine	*Kate*	*Perseus*
Helper	*Baby Fairy*	*Hermes*
Sender	*The King*	*Polydectes*
Villain	*Fairies*	*Medusa*

Why you need to know these facts

● Characterisation is a more subtle aspect of a story than the plot, but it is one that can greatly enrich reading. Teachers should take opportunities to 'flesh out' characters in the story with the children. Most texts will contain disparate facets of characterisation and the teacher is often the one best able to pull these together and bring them into a discussion with children about particular characters – what they are like, why they behave the way they do and how the children would feel if they met them.

● Empathy for characters is another one of those bridges children can use to cross from shorter stories to longer ones. By fostering their ability to empathise with a particular character and by encouraging them to track that individual through their dilemma, the teacher can further the child's capacity to sustain interest in a story.

● If children understand how characters are experienced by readers, it can help them to devise characters for their own stories. The basic set of aspects of characterisation listed above can provide children with a framework for characterising their own creations in the stories they write.

● A further aspect of children's planning of stories can be found in the area of character role. As they devise more extended stories, children should be encouraged to provide their heroes and heroines with sidekicks to help them along. Certainly there is much to be enjoyed in devising a really mean villain.

Characterisation – the process by which a story builds up a picture of a character.
Direct characterisation – direct presentation of information about a character in a text.
Indirect characterisation – the use of diverse features such as the actions or speech to build up an overall picture of a character.
Roles – different parts characters play in the events of a story.
Traits – features of characters.

Vocabulary

The way someone in a story is referred to can also help with characterisation. This is put to interesting effect by Roald Dahl. For example, in *Matilda* Matilda's father is constantly referred to as 'the father'. The impersonal use of 'the' before 'father' contrasts with another Dahl novel, *Danny, the Champion of the World* in which Danny's loving parent is usually referred to warmly as 'my father'.

Amazing facts

Children are sometimes tempted to go one character too many when writing their stories. In story writing they will often list a load of characters in the opening of a story and never use half of them. Encourage children to limit themselves to the bear minimum of characters, only introducing a new one if they really need him or her in the story.

Common misconceptions

● Collecting characters is a good starting point for heightening children's awareness of this aspect of story. As the class shares in the reading of stories, list the names of the characters on the board to enhance their understanding of the text. They can also undertake shared writing tasks in which they make an inventory of characters they know. This is a very broad heading and could go on forever but can be narrowed to become a list of:

– Villains and their sidekicks
– Characters who are not the main character in their story
– Characters who appear in more than one story
– Characters with special powers and abilities.

● Key questions about a character can unpack some of their main traits. These can be specific to a character, such as 'Why is Something Else called by that name?' or they can be general questions that could apply to a range of characters. For example:

– What do they do?
– What is done to them?
– What do they say?
– What do they think/feel?
– What do they look like?
– Where do they appear?

Questions like these can be shared in discussion. Alternatively, they can be written on cards and children can put them to each other as a preparatory discussion before writing about a particular character.

● Get the children to write letters to characters asking them questions, giving opinions on their actions and offering them advice. Variations on this include scripting a phone conversation between themselves and the character, typing out imaginary e-mail exchanges and using rectangles of card to draw and write out postcards from the character. This sort of idea can vary further into wedding invitations from Cinderella and a whole host of mail to fill the Jolly Postman's bag!

● Empathising with characters is an essential part of children's experience of literature. Get one child to take on the role of a character. Encourage the rest of the class or a smaller group to put questions to that child. To make this more supportive two children can share the task of answering for the character.

● Devising characters can involve using the forms of indirect characterisation outlined on pages 18–19. Ask the children to devise a character, bearing each of those in mind. In extended story writing they can also look at the idea of character role and assess whether their story needs characters fitting each of the roles.

Settings

The setting is the location in which a story is set. It is the backdrop against which the events of a story take place and the places through which the story moves. It can be made up of:

Subject facts

● **Named places**, whether they be familiar to the reader or not. Settings can include places known from the real world, fictitious places in the real world or places in imaginary lands.

● **Identifiable locations**, such as a kitchen, a castle or a haunted house. In each of these the reader can conjure up an image of the setting by thinking of places known from real life or other stories.

● **Descriptive text** painting a word picture of the setting and indicating objects that make up the scene, so a description of a castle may include the mention of an archway or a well.

● **The people at the location**. The characters are the people who participate in the story. However, a setting might include a number of people. For example, a football match conjures up the image of a crowd of people, within which the events of a story could evolve.

The function of settings
Settings can confuse readers. Passages in which the narrator of a story enters a 'glade with an overhanging yew to the left bordered by a row of dahlias at the side of which there was a fountain' can puzzle a reader, either because of the use of unfamiliar details or the ambiguous way in which they are set out. On the other hand, readers can easily skip through the description of a setting, hungry to read what

happened there. There is a balance readers strike here. Readers will take in the bare bones of a setting and then their concept of the setting will be influenced by more descriptive language, although they will not necessarily remember the details. As readers, we tend to develop a sense of which details we need to keep in our minds as material that will affect our appreciation of the story.

Settings can function in three significant ways:

● **Settings contribute to the mood of a story.** For example, the opening lines of *Something Else* place him 'On a windy hill alone with nothing to be friends with' and in doing so create the mood of isolation. The enhancing of a mood is a crucial function of setting. It is possible for a reader to envisage a creepy castle in a story without having been given any description. However, when Catherine Fisher describes the castle in *The Snow-Walker's Son* the castle then contributes to the way the reader feels about the characters who live there and the events that will take place in those passageways.

● **Settings can present material that affects the action of a story.** In some stories the setting plays a part in the action of the story, for example the Beanstalk in 'Jack and the Beanstalk'. Jack climbs it, cuts it down and kills the giant with it. In quest stories, the location of the story is itself a challenge the characters must solve to survive. For example, in *Dakota of the White Flats,* by Philip Ridley, the characters must make a perilous crossing of the canal, hopping from shopping trolley to shopping trolley. Dangerous settings inject action to a story. The genre of the action film, with which many children are very familiar, involves taking a relatively plain setting, such as an office block or a bus, and allowing the setting to lend all the dangerous potential latent within it to the action of a tale. In *Rosie's Walk,* by Pat Hutchins, the fox pursuing Rosie is continually thwarted by various inanimate objects placed around the farmyard.

● **Settings locate a story**. This can be a general type of place, such as a prison or restaurant. It can also be more specific, rooting the story in a place and time. The Victorian diary featured in *The Lottie Project*, by Jacqueline Wilson, indicates to the reader where and when a story is taking place. In historical fiction this is a vital aspect of setting, engaging the reader's previous knowledge of a time and place as part of the act of reading a story.

● Teachers should be aware of the challenges that settings of stories present to young readers. Children need encouragement to take in a certain amount of scene setting material, particularly noticing how an awareness of the setting can contribute to an understanding of the action. Children need to develop a healthy grasp of, but not be hung up on, the outlining of setting as their reading progresses.

Why you need to know these facts

● Children should be encouraged to set the scene in their own writing. The setting can often stimulate ideas for the rest of the story. If children devise a map of an interesting setting it can act as a stimulus for a story of a journey through the setting. As their writing develops the children should be encouraged to include descriptive detail. If they set their story in a creepy castle they need to conjure up descriptive ways of presenting that scene to the reader.

● The comparing and contrasting of settings is an activity children can begin early in their reading development. Unlike characters, settings are so prevalent throughout a story, that children can quickly see links and differences between one setting and another. This can involve looking at two settings within a story or different settings in different stories. As they do this, children will develop their critical skills of looking at features within and between stories as well as contributing to the development of their own reading preferences for stories set in particular places.

Mood – atmosphere or feeling conjured up in a story.
Setting – the location, place or time, in which a story is set.

Vocabulary

● Get the children to create a detailed map of the location of the story they are reading. The children should draw a picture of the place and add in little details they encounter as they read through the text. The children will be using drawing as a way of note-taking details from what they have read. They could produce a 3D model of the place in which a story takes place.

Teaching ideas

● Mapping out a setting can provide a stimulus to writing. This can either be a bird's-eye view of the setting or a cross-section of the different floors of a creepy house or decks of a pirate ship. After placing different details into a setting, children can devise a story that takes them through the setting, using the map as a planning tool. Notes about the story can be written on the map they have devised.

● Strip settings are a variation on the mapping idea above. Give the children a long strip of paper and ask them to use it either to note the different locations visited in a story they have read or to plan the places a story of their own will visit as it progresses. Ask the children to make notes about events along the strip. Pieces can be added at the end or, if a chunk has been missed out or children want to insert a bit, they can cut into the strip and insert a section.

● Get the children to use an adventure grid, like the one shown below, to analyse the settings they have encountered and to devise examples of their own. The setting is entered and the danger it presents noted in the second column. The 'wordbank' column provides a place for children to note vocabulary that could be useful in this activity. It could include verbs to describe the action that will take place or adjectives describing the situation. A possible solution to the danger can be added in the last column.

Setting	Danger	Wordbank	Solution
rope bridge	falling to pieces	swaying vertico ravine	run very fast

● Compare different settings within a story. Divide the class into two and give each side the description of a different setting from a story. After discussion, ask one side to say something about its setting to which the other side will respond. For example, if one side has read about Max's house in *Where the Wild Things Are*, they may have noticed that the house is fairly bare. The other side, having looked at the land of the wild things, could reply that, while there is not much furniture there it is full of leaves and waves... The other side can then respond to this.

Themes

The term *theme* is somewhat ambiguous. It is used to refer to significant ideas or issues the reader encounters in a text. For example, the story of the 'Ugly Duckling' tells of a duckling, rejected by a family, who later becomes a swan. At no point does the story state that it is about loneliness or rejection, yet these are the sorts of themes readers perceive in the story. Such themes are a matter of interpretation. The film director Woody Allen has made light of the idea of an 'author's message' by flashing these words on the screen at the point in a film when a character comes to a moment of self-discovery. However, texts tend not to overtly point out *the* theme of a story. The usual practice is that readers read a text and detect certain themes within a story. So readers might see themes of wildness and imagination in *Where the Wild Things Are* or themes of loneliness and friendship in *Something Else.*

Looking through a basket of picture books or a shelf of children's novels, a range of themes emerge that are common in children's literature, including the following list of ten common themes (obviously, these themes are not exclusive to children's literature):

- being in trouble
- discovery
- embarrassment
- fear
- growing up
- hardship
- magic
- quests
- relationships
- time

While the list of themes is potentially endless there are three broad themes that emerge in a number of children's stories. The categorising of stories as 'already there', 'journey to' and 'encounter with' are extremely broad but can help to see common concerns or ideas emerging across the range of children's literature.

'Already there' stories
'Already there' stories include those in which children come to terms with the situations in which they find themselves.

These include stories in which children negotiate their way through friendships and relationships. In *Willy the Wimp*, by Anthony Browne, a character comes to terms with himself and the bullies around him. *The Friends*, by Rosa Guy, is a powerful account of two girls and their tough New York childhood. The 'Alfie' stories of Shirley Hughes take a young child through experiences such as a first visit to a birthday party, or a first pair of wellingtons. Anne Fine has written excellent examples of stories in which characters come to terms with marital break-up and step-parents.

'Journey to' stories

'Journey to' stories is a clear and very common category. In such stories the reader follows the characters on a quest to obtain, reach or discover something. The journeys in *Where the Wild Things Are*, by Maurice Sendak, *The Neverending Story*, by Michael Ende, *The Lion, the Witch and the Wardrobe*, by CS Lewis and *The Hobbit*, by JRR Tolkein are all examples of quests. Indeed, it is such a common structure in children's literature that it is rare to visit a children's book shop and look at the table of best-selling titles without encountering a story involving the progress of a character in a quest.

'Encounter with' stories

'Encounter with' stories involve characters in the task of coming to terms with someone or something out of the ordinary, invading and disrupting their regular world. *Something Else* sees the miserable loneliness of the central character invaded by a friend; in *Harvey Angell*, by Diana Hendry, there is a similar invasion of loneliness by an angelic visitor. The visitors don't need to be animate. Into this category we could place *The Secret Garden,* by Frances Hodgson Burnett, in which the characters discover a 'magical' garden that was always within their reach and which changes their lives. Encounters can also be with parallel worlds, visitors from another time or involve the bringing of magic into this world.

It is clear that stories don't exclusively adopt one of these three themes, for example there is a sense in which *Where the Wild Things Are* includes all three: Max 'journeys to' the land where he 'encounters' the wild things, though it could be said this takes place within his bedroom and he is 'already there'. They serve as thematic guidelines rather than rigid rules.

● Themes are an essential planning tool. A familiarity with the themes of a book will enable the teacher to ensure a range of stories are read. Some readers prefer the 'journey to' type of story. However, a year spent reading only these would be an unhealthy diet. Perceiving a range of themes can inform planning the diet of literature used in class.

● Themes provide an excellent basis for discussion. By appreciating just how heavy the atmosphere of loneliness is at the start of a story like *Something Else* the teacher has found a touchstone from which to lead a discussion about why Something Else was lonely. What must he have felt like when the other creatures sent him away? Would he have tried to make friends again?

● Themes can provide a deeper focus for writing activities linked to a story. The use of a story as a stimulus can sometimes wear a bit thin and fail to fund children's imaginations. The idea of reading a story like *Farmer Duck* then asking the children to 'write a story about a nasty farmer' will often lead to thirty reproductions of the original. If, however, children are asked to think of their own story about a bully and how the bully is dealt with, the broader theme can stimulate a more varied set of ideas.

● The broad themes outlined above can serve as a planning tool in children's story writing. Children can ask themselves which of the three types of story they think their story will be. This shouldn't restrict them or tie them down but it does enable them to connect their writing activity with other texts they have experienced in that same category.

Theme – important ideas or issues in a text.

CS Lewis didn't begin the Narnia stories with the idea of a journey into the wardrobe. The stories began with an image he had of a faun carrying presents through a snowy wood. It was from this interesting image that the whole Narnia idea developed.

Understanding stories

It is worth avoiding the idea that the author meant a story to be about a particular theme. Nothing kills appreciation of a good story more than being told 'it's about loneliness' or some discussion on what the author 'meant' by a particular story. That sort of statement teaches a poor understanding of just how much various readers can get out of a story. Teaching will involve sharing some of the thematic material, but to distil a great story into a simple statement of what it is 'about' is a pitfall to avoid.

Teaching ideas

● Let the children loose on a range of stories they know well – these could be from the school library, the book corner, comic box or their own video collections. Ask them to gather three stories and to list as many common elements as they can between the three stories. If children can work with partners who also know these stories, the activity works much better.

● Comparing the treatment of themes in a range of stories can show the different ways in which similar themes are treated. For example, the theme of bullying is treated differently in *Chicken,* by Alan Gibbons, from the way it is treated in *The Eighteenth Emergency,* by Betsy Byars. While both are aimed at similar age groups and share this common theme the differences involve the way humour is used and the attitudes the characters adopt to the problem.

Resources

Stories
The list of children's stories is so extensive it is impossible to provide anything like a list of recommended titles or authors. The following list includes titles referred to extensively throughout this chapter as titles worth looking at for the way in which they use so many of the features of stories dealt with above to the fullest:

Voices in the Park, by Anthony Browne (Doubleday)
Willy the Wimp, by Anthony Browne (Walker Books)
Something Else, by Kathryn Cave (Puffin Books)
The Snow-Walker's Son, by Catherine Fisher (Red Fox)
Rosie's Walk, by Pat Hutchins (Red Fox)

Dakota of the White Flats, by Philip Ridley (Puffin Books)
Krindlekrax, by Philip Ridley (Red Fox)
Harry Potter and the Philosopher's Stone, by JK Rowling (Bloomsbury)
Where the Wild Things Are, by Maurice Sendak (Puffin Books)
Farmer Duck, by Martin Waddell (Walker Books)
The Lottie Project, by Jacqueline Wilson (Yearling Books)

About stories

These titles deal with the subject of stories, analysing aspects such as events and characters and looking at how readers respond to them:

Reading and Responding to Fiction: classroom strategies for developing literacy, by Huw Thomas (Scholastic)
Read On: Using fiction in the Primary School, by Stuart Marriott (Paul Chapman)

Working with stories

Picture Books for the Literacy Hour, by Guy Merchant and Huw Thomas (David Fulton)
Cracking Good Books: teaching literature at Key Stage 2, by Judith Graham (NATE)

These titles provide a range of practical ways of engaging with ideas covered in this chapter. The former ranges across Key Stages, advocating the use of picture books right up to year 6 while the latter focuses on Key Stage 2.

The *Read and Respond* series of books, published by Scholastic, provide various titles linked to tried and tested titles. Each title provides a range of photocopiable materials.

Writing stories

The *Writing Guides* series of books, published by Scholastic, provide focused teaching, each book clarifying the features of a different genre such as Sci-Fi stories, Recounts, Fairy Tales and Scary stories.

Chapter 2
The range of fiction

'Variety is the spice of life' and this is true in literature as in living. An essential foundation for good teaching of fiction requires a knowledge about the features of stories. This must be complemented by a working knowledge of the range of fiction children should encounter in the primary school. The widest range of fiction should be presented to children so they can develop a broad awareness of literature and develop their personal tastes.

Choosing a book

Subject facts

Competent readers develop certain tastes. They know what they like to read and they have a certain set of criteria they apply to books as they browse through in a bookshop or library. The old saying 'You can't tell a book by its cover' may contain a kernel of wisdom but the fact remains that the cover offers up a lot of information and will guide the reader in the process of making a choice. The various features of the cover provide the reader with a way of considering a book and deciding whether to read it. It both lures and informs the reader. Look at any children's book and look at the front and back cover. It will probably have on it such elements as:

- **Title.** As well as indicating what the book is about the title can add intrigue. A title such as *I was a Rat!* causes the reader to wonder who is speaking and what has led to such a statement.

- **Author's name.** The name of a well-known author such as Jacqueline Wilson can give a book automatic appeal.

- **Publisher's logo.** The logo of the company that pays for the book to be printed and distributed.

- **Picture/design.** The cover of a book will be designed to appeal to the type of reader that the publisher thinks will most enjoy the book. The style of the cover will also indicate whether the book is funny, romantic or scary and so on. The image on the cover will be chosen to hook the reader. It will say something about the story, but it will also conceal so much more. The picture by Chris Riddell on the first-ever cover of *Meteorite Spoon,* by Philip Ridley, showed two children in oversized jumpers fleeing a volcano. The image gave something away about the story – but so much was missing to intrigue the reader.

- **Blurb**. The back cover will often contain a short paragraph that gives a flavour of the book. It could be a brief introduction, written by the publishers, to the dilemmas characters will face in the story. It could be a passage quoted from the story or the words a character will say. It could be a series of questions designed to intrigue the reader: the blurb for *I was a Rat!,* by Philip Pullman, asks, 'What is he now? A terrifying monster rampaging in the sewers?'

- **Review notices.** Short snippets from reviews sometimes feature on the back cover of the paperback edition of a book. A hardback might have reviews of previous titles by the author.

- **Awards and nominations.** Information about any awards, such as the Smarties Prize or the Carnegie Medal, that the book has been nominated for or awarded will be clearly flagged on the cover. Publishers might also display the fact that the author has won an award for another book.

- **Price and ISBN number.** The price of the book and the book's unique ISBN number (both as a number and a bar code) will be printed on the back of the book.

● **Author blurb.** Information about the author can be gathered from the short biographies that are sometimes included in the inside covers of books.

● As they develop the ability to choose the material they will read, children will begin to use covers to help them make effective choices.

● Review notices and blurbs are two interesting text examples of how the ideas that contribute to a story or the opinions of a reader of a story can be expressed.

● Authors play an important role in encouraging young readers. As they develop the taste for particular writers, children will be drawn to other titles by the same author. The success of writers like Roald Dahl or Enid Blyton in part rests upon the fact that children develop an awareness of the author. Contemporary examples like Paul Jennings or Jacqueline Wilson have established names that children remember and seek out. Knowing about authors enables children to develop and follow their personal preferences.

This is a parody of a blurb written by the poet Wendy Cope for her book *Making Cocoa for Kingsley Amis*:

Brilliant, original, irreverent, lyrical, feminist, nostalgic, pastoral, anarchic, classical, plangent, candid, witty – these are all adjectives and some of them can truthfully be used to describe Wendy Cope's poems. Very few people bother to read the second sentence of a blurb. Or the third. Most of them skip to the end where it says something like this: a truly spectacular debut, an unmissable literary event.

Unfortunately, this version didn't make it to the actual back cover!

● Get the children to produce their own covers for stories they have written. This can involve making up a blurb, deciding on a cover image and even drawing a bar code. Older children should be encouraged to take time over choosing a cover image. Tell them that the picture should have that dual role of showing readers so much but making them want to find out more.

POCKET GUIDES: UNDERSTANDING TEXTS

● Blurb writing can provide an activity in itself. Get the children to read a range of blurbs and look at the way they represent stories, including features like the use of questions noted earlier. Using these tactics children can try making their own examples for stories they have read.

● Researching authors can provide a way for children to explore particular writers they enjoy. Information about authors can be gathered from the short biographies that are sometimes included in the inside covers of books, from articles such as the interviews in the magazine *Books for Keeps* or a book such as *Talking Books* (see Resources on page 54). Publisher catalogues may provide pictures of authors or their work. It is also worth contacting publishers who may have publicity material promoting a particular writer. Author posters provide a way in which children can show information about a writer. Provide the children with large sheets of paper, felt-tipped pens and pictures and materials cut out of publisher's promotional literature. Tell the children to design a poster showing facts, pictures and reviews dealing with the life and work of a particular writer.

● Reading sessions should make room for the comparison between texts by the same author or between the work of two different authors. The former is particularly important for children who are devouring every work by a single writer. They should be encouraged to pick out the particularities of each work as well as seeing the shared elements they like about the titles. Investigate with the children how a particular author revisits a particular theme, for example Martin Waddell's use of animals in stories or the way Jacqueline Wilson presents children at the cutting edge of some of life's challenges.

Narration

Authors write stories; readers read them. Between these two poles every text has a voice. This is known as the narrative voice; it is the voice of the story being told.

Subject facts

The narrative voice can be in the first person or in the third person. It can be clearly linked to one character, or it can be a more distant and objective voice. There are times when that voice speaks clearly. Narration may be overt, in the sense that the narrative voice makes it clear it is there. It can also be covert, not drawing attention to itself.

First person narration

Charles Dickens's novel *David Copperfield* is told with a simple first person narrative voice. From the first line of the novel David Copperfield is narrating his life story:

> *Whether I shall turn out to be the hero of my own life, or whether that station will be held by anyone else, these pages must show.*

The narrative voice is personal, immediate and overt. It is 'me' talking about 'my' story.

Third person narrative

One of the distinctions readers quickly detect in a story is between narration in the first and third person. The quotation above from *David Copperfield* is in the first person; David is recounting his own story. If the opening had read:

> *Whether David will turn out to be the hero of his own life, or whether that station will be held by anyone else, these pages must show.*

we would be dealing with a third person narrative. This third person is telling us about David, referring to 'him' and 'his' story.

Point of view

While a third person narrative is often more distant than a first person narrative, it is equally possible that a third person narrative may capture the emotion and feeling surrounding the events recounted in a tale. The text can also lead the reader to understand what is taking place from a particular point of view. This term, *point of view*, is used in literary theory to describe the perspective from which the action of a story is being presented.

In a moving passage in Jan Mark's *The Snow Maze*, the narrator presents the feelings of the bullied child, Joe, as he weighs up the nature of the bully alongside Irrum, the girl who has stuck up for him.

> *Joe did not want to be like Akash, big and strong. He wanted to be like Irrum, small and brave.*

Grammatically, the text is in the distant and objective third person, but look at the ease with which it can slip into a first person narrative:

*I did not want to be like Akash, big and strong. I wanted
to be like Irrum, small and brave.*

Such a smooth transition illustrates that the earlier version,
though it is grammatically in the third person, still carries
the central character's feelings and insights as much as if it
were written in the first person. The text is written from
Joe's point of view.

In this quote from *Clockwork*, by Philip Pullman, the text
is told from Gretl's point of view:

*Gretl could only stare: in horror at Sir Ironsoul and his
sword, in wonder at the prince.*

Such passages cause the reader to enter into the feelings of
a particular character. Here, the reader sees with Gretl's
eyes, feels the horror looking in one direction and wonder
looking in the other.

Overt and covert voices
There are times in a story when a narrator, though writing
in the third person, discloses its voice. Martin Waddell's
beautiful book, *The Hidden House*, tells the story of three
dolls left on the window ledge of an abandoned woodland
cottage. When there are human characters in the story the
narrative voice is covert; it just recalls the humans' thoughts
and the actions. But, whenever the human characters are
absent, a narrative voice becomes overt to proffer insights
into the unspoken thoughts of the dolls:

*Maisie Ralph and Winnaker watched [the decay of the old
house] happen... until the spiders spun up their window so
that there was nothing left to see but webs. They didn't say
anything, because they were wooden dolls, but I think
they were lonely.*

The 'I' who thinks is the overt narrator's voice.

Narrative privilege
To a greater or lesser degree the narrative voice knows
things that you or I would not have seen had we been
watching the events. In *The Snow Maze*, we wouldn't have
seen how Joe felt, but the narrative voice can tell us. In
literary theory, this is called narrative privilege. The
narrator is privileged, knowing things you or I would not
have seen as eyewitnesses. The narrator can disclose
thoughts and feelings and be all-knowing.

Unreliable narrator

You can't always trust narrators. It is possible to encounter an unreliable narrator who will skew the story in a particular direction. There are a number of examples in children's literature of children who narrate a story in a way that gives their own spin on events, for example in *The Story of Tracy Beaker* by Jacqueline Wilson.

Why you need to know these facts

● Identifying the role of the narrator in the communication process builds the ability of young readers to understand what is going on in a story. The use of 'I' in a story should prompt them to ask 'Who is this *I* ?' and to form some opinions about the voice doing the telling.

● Narration is an important aspect of writing. As they encounter different sorts of narrative voice children can try developing the use of narrative voices in their own stories. Primarily they need to realise that the voice that says 'I' in a story doesn't need to be them. Once they realise this they can enjoy taking on other personalities and telling different stories in different roles.

● An understanding of the varying points of view involved in stories can be engendered by the teacher when reading with children. It is up to the teacher to root out the sorts of verbal details that indicate the narrator's point of view. Ask the children questions about how a few different characters feel about events being recalled. Look out for feeling words such as 'sad' or 'scared'. Look out for references to what characters 'saw' and ask the children to picture what it would look like to that character.

● The children's opinions and feelings can be critically refined by considering the different ways in which various characters would have viewed events in a story. Children can begin to pick apart events in a story, considering how they would have seemed from different points of view. This should be accompanied by a consideration of the point of view that is dominant within the text. Through such consideration children can develop a critical attitude to the actual narrator. So, when reading *The Story of Tracy Beaker*, children can reflect critically on the narrator, Tracy, who often presents a one-sided picture of events. Children can begin to infer what actually is taking place in the life of this unreliable narrator realising, for example that her attacks of hay fever are the times when she is actually crying.

Covert narration – narration where the narrative voice is not obvious.

First person narration – the telling of a story in the voice of one of the main characters in the story, for example 'I saw Natalie and we went shopping'.

Narrative privilege – the way in which the narrative voice can relate things a pure observer would not have seen, such as how a particular character was feeling.

Narrator – the voice that 'tells' a story.

Overt narration – times when the narrative voice becomes more obvious.

Point of view – the presentation of events from the viewpoint of a particular character.

Third person narration – story told in the voice of someone removed from the events, for example 'He saw Natalie and they went shopping'.

Unreliable narrator – a narrator whose record of events is unreliable – possibly due to opinion or bias.

There is a common misconception that third person writing is more objective. Just as a first person narrator will tell the story from their point of view, a third person narrator can actually be presenting events from the point of view of one specific character.

● Diaries provide an opportunity for children to experiment with the idea of first person narration. By writing a diary of a narrator removed from themselves, such as an alien or an insect, children can relate events in the narrative voice of their chosen character. Ask the children to write a diary for one of the characters in a book they have read. In the diary form they can recall events that happen on different days.

● Collect examples of texts and paragraphs that have interesting uses of the narrative voice or of point of view. Look for examples of overt narration or narrative privilege. Give the texts to the children and ask them to investigate the different ways in which the stories are narrated.

● Retelling a story from an alternative point of view is a common enough task. Children are often encouraged to tell a story like that of Theseus from the point of view of the Minotaur. However, this sort of activity needs to take place in a context where there is some guidance as to how to present a point of view.

Children should be encouraged to:

– relate what the character sees as different events take place, using different words for 'see' such as 'glimpsed' and 'noticed'.

– use adjectives that show how certain things would have appeared from their character's point of view, such as the use of 'cosy' to describe the 'Labyrinth' in a story told from the Minotaur's point of view.

– use the words to indicate a character's point of view, so instead of writing about 'the heroic Theseus' the Minotaur might refer to 'the irritating young hooligan with a big ball of string'.

● Hot-seating is a way of exploring the events of a story as seen from the point of view of a particular character. Ask one child to volunteer to be in the hot seat. Ask your volunteer to sit in front of the rest of the class and pretend to be a particular character from a book the class know well. Encourage the rest of the class to ask the child questions about their character. For example the child may take on the role of Gretl in *Clockwork*, by Philip Pullman, in which case another child could ask 'How did you feel as you climbed the stairs?' The child in the hot seat must answer as Gretl, for example 'I was scared but I...'

Genre

Subject facts

Texts can be sorted into groupings that share a familial likeness. Stories set in futuristic space settings show some resemblance to each other and can be grouped into the familial cluster of 'science fiction' stories. These familial groupings are the genres of texts. Horror stories, adventure stories, historical fiction – these are all examples of commonly referred to genres. There is no hard and fast set of genres that exist in literature.

Genres are formed from two processes. Firstly there is the historical development of texts that spring from the same family. If I sit down to write a murder story, including clues and a detective who solves them I will be writing within a genre of mystery stories or detective fiction. It is a genre with a long ancestry running through the work of Agatha Christie and Sir Arthur Conan Doyle back to a writer like Wilkie Collins. In following the conventions of the genre, I help to define them.

The other side of this process is the way in which readers choose and organise their reading according to such familial groupings. From my own experience as a child who didn't read much, it was from interest in the work of one writer of detective fiction that I began to read others. Like many readers I found one member of the family and allowed the resemblance to guide me in the reading of others. This double process of where the texts are coming from and how they are reaching their destination creates the dynamics by which genres are formed.

This short catalogue of genres notes some of the main ones with which primary teachers should aim to familiarise themselves:

Fairy tales

Fairy tales are set in an unnamed place, usually with an older feel to the environment. They include traditional characters such as witches and princesses and involve magical events such as spells or talking animals. One feature to look out for in a fairy tale is the 'rule of three' – an action will often be repeated three times, or the hero asked to choose between three options. For example, Jack has three visits up the Beanstalk and Goldilocks encounters three situations in the house of the Three Bears.

There are numerous fairy tale collections available and many retellings of classic stories (see Resources on page 55).

Familiar setting stories

These include stories set in locations children know from their daily routine, for example schools or streets. Such stories find features of the familiar setting, such as the loss of a toy or a dilemma with a friend, and develop the situation into a storyline.

Good examples can be found in the work of Shirley Hughes. Her titles tend to involve schools, children's parties, local parks and jumble sales.

Fantasy stories

Fantasy stories are set in parallel settings to our own world. They often inhabit lands that are mapped out by the author and feature fantastic places and creatures. There is often an element of a quest to such stories, in which the characters have to journey through various settings and encounter certain objects to accomplish a particular goal.

Stories such as *The Lion, the Witch and the Wardrobe,* by CS Lewis, and *The Neverending Story,* by Michael Ende, are examples of such parallel worlds in which new and fantastic situations emerge. In both stories, the children from this world venture into the other world.

Science fiction stories

Science fiction stories are also set in fantastic settings but the settings for science fiction stories are usually ones that are futuristic or extraterrestrial. Such stories often involve technological or scientific features such as spaceships or time machines. They may include journeys to other planets, aliens and futuristic settings.

This genre lacks a significant number of enduring stories for children. In some, for example *Spacebaby*, by Henrietta Branford, there is the classic visitor from another planet. In terms of investing stories with scientific ideas the *Uncle Albert* books by Russell Stannard provide entertaining stories based around the ideas of Albert Einstein.

Adventure and mystery stories

Adventure and mystery stories involve characters in some sort of crime or quest. The characters may need to solve a crime or get themselves out of some sort of trouble. The stories are often exciting and have atmospheres and plots that keep the reader wanting to find out what happened next. Children wanting to read this type of story could be directed towards the *Goosebumps* series of scary stories, or to the excellent thriller *Operation Gadgetman!* by Malorie Blackman. Older children can try the *Sherlock Holmes* stories.

Historical stories

Historical stories are, as the name implies, set in the past. Settings such as Roman or Tudor times have proven popular with writers of such works. Good writers in this area manage to conjure up a feel for the period and bring in detail about the time. There will often be a clear adventure story and the best historical fiction avoids the trap of just providing historical detail.

Terry Deary's *Tudor Terror* series manages to include a lot of information about historical figures and background information about life in Tudor times. In a *Tudor Terror* story the reader will find:

- accurate background detail
- mention of historical events from the time of the story
- walk-on parts for historical characters
- mystery that draws on Tudor politics.

Some modern writers have tackled the harder themes of history, such as child labour in *Street Child,* by Berlie Doherty, or slavery in *Whose Side are You on?* by Alan Gibbons.

Issues raising or dilemma stories

This one of those catch-all terms that includes such a diversity of texts it seems a bit of a cheat to call it a genre. However there are a large number of children's books that deal with situations such as family separation, bereavement or the experience of being in care.

There was a spate of books some years ago with titles such as *Shaun's Family is Dysfunctional* that tended to be worthy and preachy, but writers such as Jacqueline Wilson and Anne Fine have managed to produce work on subjects such as step-parenting, divorce, a mum getting a new partner or children who do 'evil' things, in a way that is refreshingly honest and gripping.

Traditional stories – myths, legends, fables, parables

This heading covers a variety of different types of story, ranging from the alternative world views of myths to the small scale on which fables appear. This area is dealt with in the following section.

Identifying genre

The features of the different genres are open to investigation. As they read a mystery story encourage them to look to see what gives it a particular generic identity. Ask them to pick out the elements from the initial chapter of a book. For example, the discovery of the initial crime scene with its suspicious letter in *Operation Gadgetman!* provides a short example of the gradual realisation that all is not well and the use of clues to figure things out.

There are obvious features of genres, such as the inclusion of gore and horror in some suspense stories. But there are more subtle features that re-appear in story after story, such as the locked room that holds a secret which won't be disclosed for a good few chapters or the suspense with which a character makes her or his way through a setting. Such refinements can feed into children's planning of their own stories.

In her book, *Genre* (Methuen), Heather Dubrow has a fascinating way of showing how readers are influenced by their expectations of a text's genre. Her study of genre opens with the following passage which she asks us to assume is from a novel called *Murder at Marplethorpe*. It opens:

*The clock on the mantelpiece said ten thirty but someone
had suggested recently that the clock was wrong. As the
figure of the dead woman lay on the bed in the front
room, a no less silent figure glided rapidly from the
house. The only sounds to be heard were the ticking of a
clock and the loud wailing of an infant.*

When read as an example of a detective story the reader's
expectations home in on the clue of the clock telling the
wrong time. They assume the dead woman to be the victim.
The silent figure must be a murderer. Dubrow then asks
her readers to reread the passage, this time reading it as if
it was from a 'formation novel' – the sort of life story that
traces the growing up of a hero (for example *David
Copperfield*). Dubrow calls this imaginary novel *The
Personal History of David Marplethorpe*. When read as an
example of this genre the clock may appear symbolic. The
dead woman is possibly the mother, tragically placed at the
start of young David Marplethorpe's life. He is probably the
crying child. The silent figure may be sending for medical
help. In both cases the different expectations are prompted
by the reader's usual expectations when reading texts in a
particular genre.

**Why you need to
know these facts**

● Planning the input made into children's reading involves
an awareness of the full range of children's literature. An
understanding of genre is essential when it comes to
resourcing a school library's fiction collection or a
classroom book corner. Catering for varying tastes should
also feature in the planning and resourcing of lessons. It is
worth aiming to use text extracts from a range of different
titles. It would be beyond the constraints of time to expect to
read a class novel from each of the genres listed above but
the potential is there to read an opening chapter or a
significant event from each. It is also worth scanning the
shelves of the local children's bookshop to keep abreast of
the different types of title emerging in each of these areas.

● The way in which certain generic character types appear
in stories such as detectives, aliens or magicians provides a
rich resource for comparison across a range of texts.

● Genres provide scope for the fostering of individual
tastes. Security in a genre can be an encouragement to read
more. Children seem to like that fact that they can perceive

certain features they read in one story appearing in another, such as the way in which a crime is often perceived to be the work of one character who emerges as an innocent heroine or hero, leaving the reader with a twist in the tale. This secure return to the familiar could account for some of the success of the *Goosebumps* series or the *Famous Five* stories by Enid Blyton.

● Genre features can stimulate writing. By gathering their ideas about how a particular genre works children can begin to see their own opportunity to write stories in a similar vein.

The term *science fiction* was coined in the late 1920s. Before that the genre had the title *scientifiction*.

Amazing facts

● Genres are not fixed, but rather change over time. Shakespeare's classic genres of tragedies and comedies embraced some varied works that may now be slotted into other genres, such as the tragedy of *Macbeth* which may these days have been filed under the heading of 'thriller' or even 'horror' story.

Common misconceptions

Genres change over time and works are constantly emerging that push at the boundaries of generic conventions, such as Umberto Eco's classic work *The Name of the Rose*, part detective story, part historical novel, part meditation on language. Such works show the way in which generic boundaries can be shifted and altered.

● Science fiction and fantasy are easily confused. While there is no hard and fast rule for distinguishing the two, a distinction can be found by looking at the subject matter of the story and asking whether they involve scientific ideas. Children's stories may contain trips to the Moon, like the one made by Baby Bear in his cardboard box in *Whatever Next!* by Jill Murphy. There may be journeys to the past but these can be by magical means, as in *The Secret of the Indian,* by Lynne Reid Banks. These are magical stories but don't really count as science fiction. If the events of the story have a technical or scientific feel, taking spaceships into space or time machines to the past, then they do.

The range of fiction

● Genre names should be introduced from an early stage. Children should be taught to recognise the difference between 'scary books' and 'funny books'. *I Like Books*, by Anthony Browne can provide children with an early introduction to the range of types of story available. The terminology isn't an end in itself. Genre terminology can provide children with a map of literature, enabling them to chart their book preferences and reading choices.

● The ideas that the name of a particular genre evokes can be investigated using a Genregram. Place a genre title at the centre of a piece of paper and ask the children to write ideas that they associate with the genre around it. A group of Year 6 children were asked to consider the genre of 'mystery' and devised the following Genregram.

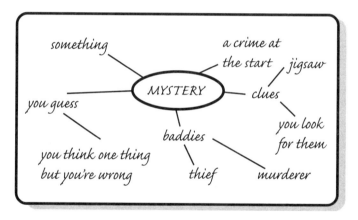

● Genres can provide material for modelling writing. In a class discussion, list the features that make up an adventure or science fiction story. The children could use a list like the one on page 42 to help them plan their own historical story.

● Encourage the children to come up with their own criteria for subdividing stories. Give small groups of children piles of about thirty books each. Ask the children to group the books into five families. Tell them to devise their own criteria for clustering the books together and to create broad titles for these families. They may come up with:
– books where something scary happens
– books with animals behaving like people
– books like real life
– books with magic in them.

Traditional stories

The umbrella term *traditional story* encompasses a range of varied types of tale. The main ones that are encountered in the primary school are:

- myth
- legend
- fable
- parable
- fairy tale.

These can be roughly classified according to certain common characteristics.

Myths
Myths are fantastical stories, often set outside the natural world as we know it. They involve stories such as the tale of Prometheus, the giant who steals fire from the gods to warm the human beings he has made. The world of such tales is a bizarre one in which gods and humans can cross between this world and another. Creation myths and other stories that explain how certain natural features came to be fall into this category.

Legends
Legends are set in a more recognisable, natural world. They involve heroic characters, set in history, often still including flights of magical fantasy but in a setting something akin to the historic. Examples such as the legends of Robin Hood or King Arthur present the reader with an embellished account of a figure who may have some historical precedent.

Fables
Fables are traditional tales that teach a lesson. They often involve animals, as in many of the fables of Aesop, and present a short narrative in which a moral is demonstrated. For example, the tale of 'The boy who cried wolf', teaches us not to raise false alarms. Characters and settings are often vague and ill-defined and the focus of the story is on the moral event being illustrated.

Parables
Parables are religious stories that illustrate a piece of spiritual teaching. Many are drawn from the teaching of Jesus in the Christian Bible, for example the 'Parable of the Good Samaritan' that shows how we should 'love our neighbour'.

Fairy tales

Fairy tales are stories collected largely within European traditions involving the magical transformation of a character's fortunes. Characters such Cinderella or the Miller's son who looked after Puss-in-Boots are protected or assisted by magic. These tales often involve characters such as kings, queens, princes, princesses, giants or fairies.

Actants and structure

Traditional tales often involve similar sets of characters. A *receiver* will be obtaining the *object* of the story – something needed or sought after, such as a golden fleece or relief from a predatory dragon. The receiver receives the object from the *subject* – another character who may be assisted by one or more *helpers*. The subject may have been sent by a *sender* – another character, such as King Minos or King Arthur, and may face an *opposer* – the villain of the piece. The narrative theorist AJ Greimas produced a diagram of these roles in his book *Structural Semantics* (see Figure 1).

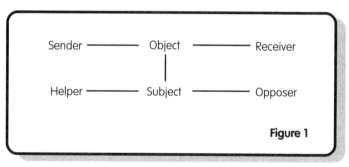

Figure 1

Into these roles it is possible to insert different names for different stories such as the fairy tale 'Kate Crackernuts' (see Figure 2) or the myth of Perseus (see Figure 3).

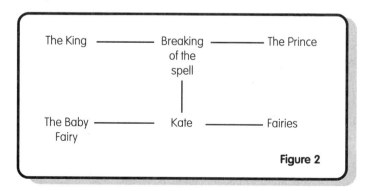

Figure 2

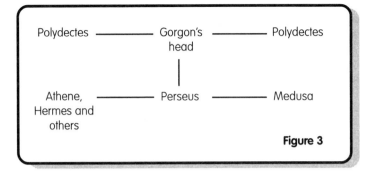

Figure 3

While not every story will have a character that neatly fills every space, this pattern offers a way of comparing and analysing traditional stories.

Motifs

There are certain motifs that occur in traditional tales. These are the traditional features or common patterns that can often be observed at work within these stories. They include:

● **A rule of three** that crops up in many traditional tales: For example, Orpheus must sing his way through three obstacles on his journey to the Underworld; in the Peruvian myth of 'The Magic Fruit', three helpers guide the magician; and in 'Kate Crackernuts', Kate makes three visits to the goblin cave.

● **Reversals** occur when the youngest and apparently least able character, triumphs, leaving the hunks behind. For example, in the Scottish legend of 'The Mester Stoorworm', the youngest son of seven strapping lads, dismissed by his father as a daydreamer, defeats a monster that stretches to the horizon. Parables also thrive on reversals – in the 'Parable of the Good Samaritan', the Samaritan, the character least expected to help, saves the traveller; in the 'Parable of the Prodigal Son', the son who has spent all his inheritance is given a joyous welcome from his father.

● **Binding and unbreakable spells** and promises can frustrate gods and kings. For example, in 'The children of Lir' the children are changed into swans which leaves the Irish god unable to undo the magic. An unbreakable promises binds Sir Gawain to having his head cut off in the legend of 'Sir Gawain and the Green Knight'.

● **Disguises and shape shifts** abound in ancient tales. In one of the legends of King Arthur, the hag Rag Nell saves the life of King Arthur on the condition that she marries Sir Gawain – who seems to get his fare share of unbreakable vows. In *The Odyssey*, Odysseus returns home disguised as a shipwrecked sailor, seeing off the suitors who seek his wife's hand in marriage.

● **Secret weaknesses of the villain are discovered** – indeed, the term 'Achilles heel' comes from a myth. In the myth of Perseus, the ocean nymphs kit Perseus out with the way to attack Medusa. In the fairy tale 'Kate Crackernuts', Kate overhears the secrets of the fairy folk, enabling her to release a spellbound Prince and restore her sheep-headed sister to normality.

Why you need to know these facts

● Traditional stories make an essential contribution to the literacy curriculum. They can be deceptively simple stories that manage to carry deep themes and engaging dilemmas. Children are often fascinated by characters' dilemmas, like Sir Gawain's promise to allow the Green Knight to behead him or the Princess's promise to give her first born to Rumpelstiltskin. These stories have lasted with reason and bring much to their readers and listeners.

● The term traditional tales is an extremely broad one and doesn't do justice the variety of stories that comes under this heading. For a full appreciation that enables a complete coverage of these types of tales the teacher needs to be aware of the subtle distinctions between myths, legends and so on.

● An understanding of some of the fantastic features and some of the patterns and motifs within traditional tales can provide the teacher with a good resource around which to build discussion of these tales. In recalling the story of 'Jack and the Beanstalk' children can be helped to remember the tale by thinking through the classic pattern of three visits. The rule of three in this story can structure discussion of the story and can provide a framework for activities, for example writing a version of the story or acting it out in three scenes.

● Motifs, patterns and characteristics of such stories are an essential tool in storytelling. Traditional tales survived centuries of being told and retold, handed down over the years, because of such patterns. The teacher who wants to tell such stories rather than just read them out of a book would do well to study the patterns as a way of remembering the detail.

The distinction between myths and legends is not always clear. Myths and legends involve varying levels of credibility, a feature that inevitably emerges in children's discussion of such stories. The stories of King Arthur can, in part, read like a historical gathering of a team of knights by a king. The Robin Hood legend would seem to have some basis in fact. A more interesting question about the veracity of such tales occurs when we look at myths. While a story such as Pandora's Box may not have a shred of historical credibility. Seen as the story of a one person's inability to resist the temptation to look in a box which she had been told never to open the tale may be seen to carry a certain moral truth!

● Give the children a selection of fairy tales and ask them to compare the motifs in them. A string of stories such as 'Snow White', 'Sleeping Beauty' and 'Jack and the Beanstalk' can result in a comparison of:
– the danger faced by the main character
– how they met the danger.
The motifs listed in this chapter can provide a focus for seeing similarities between stories.

● Brief traditional tales quickly provide a good stock of story material for children to work on. The structures of tales such as 'Puss-in-Boots' make them easy to recall in a way that enables children to represent such known stories in new ways. They can contribute illustrations to the production of a big book of a fairy tale or act out a fable in a school assembly.

● Using the idea of actants, outlined on page 48, ask the children to look at a range of stories to consider how conventional roles appear in different tales. How, for example, is the role of *hero* or *heroine* or the role of *sender* fulfilled in each story? In what ways does a *helper* contribute to the success of the *hero* or *heroine* in different stories? Ask the children to focus on one actant in particular, for example the children could analyse the role of the *helper* or the *opposer* over a range of stories. Ask the children to analyse the various reasons *senders* in a range of stories get someone else to do the task rather than tackle it themselves? The dynamics of these relationships and the ways in which various actants behave can provide a model for children when devising their own legend or fairy tale.

● Use a world map to show the children where various stories originated from. A good collection of traditional tales, such as those by Rosen and McCaughrean, (see Resources on page 55) will provide information about the origin of each story, enabling the class to mark the origin of each new story on their story map.

● Ask the children to evaluate a selection of retellings. Myths and legends often spawn a host of retellings – think how many recounts of the Minotaur story are available. Ask the children to collect a range of retellings of the same story and to look at them critically. Children should be encouraged to look at the different style each retelling adopts. Ask them to think about what sort of audience they think each particular retelling would appeal to. Ask them to evaluate how different retellings evoke different responses.

● Storytelling is a skill that every teacher should try and cultivate. Reading is important but telling has certain crucial advantages, particularly in the area of traditional tales. Storytelling is:
– suited to tales that arose from an oral background
– lively and fascinating for children, who listen in a different way to an oral narrative
– fun for the teller as they interact with the audience.
The following set of tips for telling will help in this task but the main piece of advice for any budding storyteller is 'take the plunge'. Children love storytelling as a complement to reading and it is well worth trying to learn to retell a story in a quiet part of the school where you can throw yourself fully into the tale. Storytelling tips:

1. Select your story carefully. You can't just pick up any old story and regurgitate it orally. First you need to hear the story or read it aloud from a book and recognise in it features that make it a story you could tell. Some storytellers are attracted by stories with loud sections, others by hushed and magical features.

2. When you have found a story you want to tell find the structure to it that makes it easy to recall. Many traditional

tales operate on a 'rule of three', in which something event happens three times, for example Jack's three visits up the Beanstalk.

3. Get to know the characters in the story you will tell. You need to be sure who is in the story, when you will mention them and what they will do. Knowing the difference between Athene and Arachne is a crucial part of readying yourself to tell the tale.

Giving each character a distinctive voice can spice up a telling. One way of doing this is to think of characters from films or television programmes that had particularly good voices and 'steal' these. You may not mimic them perfectly but having them in mind can be an inspiration. This explains why all my ratty kings and outwitted sheriffs rant in a voice akin to Basil Fawlty.

4. Arrange the children in a circle or a semicircle. Stand inside this circle to tell your story. Move around as you tell the story. Movement can be an excellent way of keeping children in touch with the telling of the story. I recall one teller who noticed two children whose attentions had started to wander. They were soon brought back to the action as the teller, becoming a Norse giant, thundered right beside them.

5. Involve the children. They can chime in with refrained phrases such as 'Fee, fi, fo, fum...' or join in with movements and hand actions. If Robin Hood fires an arrow, the storyteller's hand should shoot through the air. Sometimes you will need to beckon children with your hand to join in.

6. Know what response you expect different parts of the story to evoke in your audience so that you can communicate that emotion in your telling. Stories can take us from the splendour and wealth of the life of the young Buddha to the awesome moment at which, having been shielded from suffering, he first encounters it. Know and play upon the emotional content of the story you tell.

7. Props should only be used sparingly. Too many of them or the overuse of one prop can distract the listener. However, in the Cypriot tale in which an old thief ends up pulling a snake out of his bag of ill-gotten goods, the use of a long rubber snake flapping out of a bag has ended many a telling with a fine response.

Resources

Teachers working with children's literature should have some idea of the various authors whose work they could introduce within their teaching. The range of authors, the ways they write and the subjects they tackle make this an area beyond the scope of this book, however, a list of authors and titles for recommended reading is provided here.

Books about books
Talking Books, by James Carter (RoutledgeFalmer) is an edited collection of interviews and articles about popular children's authors such as Jacqueline Wilson and Philip Pullman.
I Like Books, by Anthony Browne (Walker Books) is a picture book about books, describing different genres.

Stories from various genres:

Familiar setting stories
Dogger, by Shirley Hughes (Red Fox)
Tales of Trotter Street, by Shirley Hughes (Walker Books)
Daddy Long Legs, by Anne Fine (Walker Books)
Taking the Cat's Way Home, by Jan Mark (Walker Books)

Fantasy stories
The Secret of the Indian, by Lynne Reid Banks (Collins)
Something Else, by Kathryn Cave (Puffin Books)
The Neverending Story, by Michael Ende (Puffin Books)
The Snow-Walker's Son, by Catherine Fisher (Red Fox)
The Lion, the Witch and the Wardrobe, by CS Lewis (Collins)
Whatever Next! by Jill Murphy (MacMillan)
I was a Rat! by Philip Pullman (Yearling)
Meteorite Spoon, by Philip Ridley (Puffin Books)

Science fiction stories
Spacebaby, by Henrietta Branford (Collins)
Black Holes and Uncle Albert, by Russell Stannard (Faber)

Adventure and mystery stories
Operation Gadgetman! by Malorie Blackman (Yearling)
Thief, by Malorie Blackman (Corgi)
Classic Sherlock Holmes, by Sir Arthur Conan Doyle (Scholastic)

Historical stories
Tudor Terror series, by Terry Deary (Orion)
Street Child, by Bernie Doherty (Collins)
Whose Side Are You On? by Alan Gibbons (Yearling)
Clockwork, by Philip Pullman (Yearling)

Issues raising or dilemma stories
Step By Wicked Step, by Anne Fine (Puffin Books)
The Tulip Touch, by Anne Fine (Puffin Books)
The Story of Tracey Beaker, by Jacqueline Wilson (Yearling)

Traditional tales collections
There are numerous collections of myths, fairy tales and so
on. The list below is selected to provide a good range of well
retold tales.
First Fairy Tales, by Margaret Mayo (Orchard Books)
Golden Myths and Legends of the World, by Geraldine
McCaughrean (Orion)
The Hare and the Tortoise: And Other Animal Stories, by
Sally Grindley and John Bendall-Brunello (Bloomsbury)
South and North, East and West, by Michael Rosen
(Walker Books)
Celtic Myths, by Sam McBratney (Hodder Wayland)
The Orchard Book of Greek Myths, by Geraldine
McCaughrean (Orchard Books)
The Orchard Book of Magical Tales, by Margaret Mayo
(Orchard Books)

Three Scholastic Literacy Centres deal specifically with
traditional tales. They are:
Fiction Orange: Traditional stories: aimed at year 2
(Primary 3)
Fiction Green: Myths, Fables and Legends: aimed at year 3
(Primary 4)
Fiction Purple: Myths, Fables and Legends: aimed at year 5
(Primary 6)

Chapter 3
Reading non-fiction

The differences between fiction and non-fiction texts begin, obviously, with the subject matter. Generally non-fiction is not fictitious whereas fiction is 'made up'. But that is only the start of the matter. Within non-fiction there can be texts that relate to unchallenged facts, such as the roundness of the Earth, and texts that give opinions that could be debated, such as the merits of nuclear energy. Non-fiction texts vary in their presentation and purpose, both from fiction texts and from each other, and an understanding of these differences provides an essential starting point for teaching children how to work with such texts.

Organisation of non-fiction texts

Subject facts

Types of non-fiction

A starting point for understanding how non-fiction texts work is to look at their purposes. If you make a list of the non-fiction texts you have read recently, some of them may have been recreational reading but the majority are likely to have been approached for a specific purpose, for example a recipe or an encyclopaedia. The text you are now reading is, presumably, being looked at with a view towards meeting some need and fulfilling a purpose. Other examples include texts that:

- recount events, such as history texts or newspaper articles
- report information on something, such as an outline of the features of the solar system or a guidebook on a particular place
- explain how a particular process takes place, such as a science text on the way a prism works
- give instructions on how to do something, such as a recipe book or a leaflet on assembling a piece of furniture
- discuss the two sides of a controversial issue
- aim to persuade the reader to agree with or buy into something.

The way such texts can be structured into a writing process will be examined in Chapter 4. However, the thing to note at this stage is the way that non-fiction texts are geared towards a particular purpose.

Using non-fiction

Non-fiction texts are organised in a different way to fiction. Stories tend to have a conventional beginning, middle and end and, while the reader may reread a favourite part of a story, the usual route is to begin at the beginning and progress through the storyline to the end. Non-fiction is both read and consulted. It is read through for information and can be a leisurely read, but it is also 'turned to' for reference purposes. The reader is far more likely to begin non-fiction texts at a point that matches a particular purpose. A reader wanting to know more about the country of Benin will pick up a book on Africa and begin at the appropriate section of the book. The reader might use the index to locate the page where the subject is covered. Similarly, a reader with a specific purpose will look up the same subject in a few non-fiction texts.

There is a difference in purpose between looking in a book for a specific piece of information and reading a story for pleasure. The organisational features and layout of non-fiction texts often reflect the different ways in which they are likely to be used, and often include: chapter headings, an index, a glossary, sub-headings, bullet points and lists, boxes, typographical changes and charts and diagrams. The combination of these features in a non-fiction book contribute to the breaking down of information for the reader into an accessible and manageable form.

Chapter headings

Whereas in fiction texts chapter headings, if they are used, give veiled references to the content of the chapter, in non-fiction texts clear chapter headings are used as signposts to guide the reader through the book. For example:

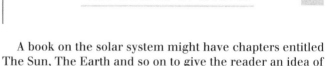

Chapter 1

The Source of a River

A book on the solar system might have chapters entitled The Sun, The Earth and so on to give the reader an idea of where to turn for information on a particular subject.

Contents page

Contents pages list the chapters and sections in a text with page numbers to guide the reader.

Index

Placed at the back of non-fiction texts, indexes list key words alongside page numbers showing where information on a particular topic can be located. For example:

picture 5, 6, 25
plot 7, 9–15, 56
poetry 21, 48
presentation 21, 25

Readers using an index need to be aware that information for one subject can be given under a range of terms, so in a book on the constitution a subject like 'queen' could be indexed under 'monarch' or 'royalty'.

Glossary

Technical or specific terms used in a non-fiction book will sometimes be gathered together in a glossary at the back of the book as a useful reference for the reader.

Qu'ran: the holy book, read by Muslims.

Sub-headings

A non-fiction chapter or page will often have information organised under separate headings, marked out by a distinctive typeface. For example the sub-headings used in this book are in a bold and slightly larger typeface than the main text.

Bullet points and listing techniques

Facts can be listed or points might be made distinct by using bullet points or other such symbol to alert the reader to the distinct identity of each fact.

The features of a castle included:
- moat
- great hall
- bailey
- keep

Boxes

Non-fiction pages will sometimes include separate boxes set within the page. These boxes might contain distinct pieces of information or a summary of information in the section.

Chapter 1

Traditional Stories

The umbrella term *traditional story* encompasses a range of varied types of tale. The main ones that are encountered in the primary school are:
- myth
- legend
- fable
- parable
- fairy tale.

These can be roughly classified according to certain common characteristics.

Myths

Myths are fantastical stories, often set outside the natural world as we know it. They involve stories such as the tale of Prometheus, the giant who steals fire from the gods to warm the human beings he has made. The world of such tales is a bizzare one in which gods and humans can cross between this world and another.

Creation myths and other stories that explain how certain natural features came to be fall into this category.

The Australian Aboriginies have a creation story which tells how the Darling River was created long ago.

Typographic changes
Bold or italic lettering is sometimes used to mark out certain words. Where books use this device the reader needs to be aware of what the typography indicates. It could mean that such a word is included in the glossary or that there is a chapter on this particular word. Alternatively it could indicate that the word is a key word within the subject matter.

Charts and diagrams
Charts and diagrams can be used to illustrate subject matter, such as a diagram of the parts of a flower. Information can also be presented in a graphic form, such as:

– a table
– a binary key: a chart that subdivides categories using a tree structure in which categories branch into sub-categories
– a spidergram: a chart that elaborates the various pieces of information stemming from a subject
– a route diagram: a chart that connects various pieces of information in a sequence.

Table

	Structure	Language features
Recount texts	orientation events conclusion language features	specific participants past tense
Instruction texts	a goal materials step-by-step directions hints conclusion	imperative verbs simple present tense step-by-step connecting words prepositions
Report texts	general presentation particular summary	present tense generalised participants linking verbs formal and objective tone

Binary key

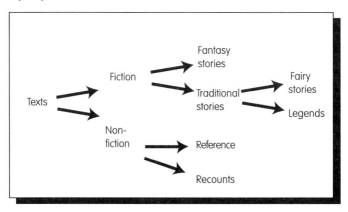

Spidergram

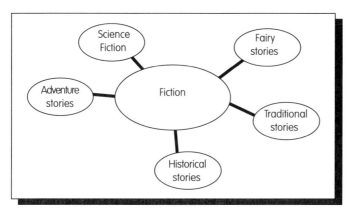

Route diagram

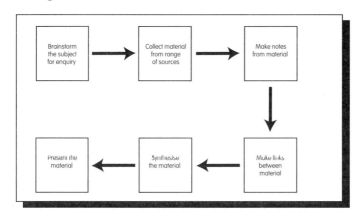

Reading non-fiction

Chart and diagram reading can be enhanced by encouraging children to focus on three questions when they encounter a graphic feature:

- What facts can you see?
- What routes do we use?
- What connections can you make?

The 'facts' question is straightforward enough. In early encounters with such features, children need time to just try and pick out some facts, such as terms they recognise or units in which measurements are given.

The 'routes' question involves recognising the directions in which charts such as tables are read. This can involve reading across a row or down a column, following the flow of arrows or recognising where two paths branch out.

The 'connections' question brings the above together. Following the route between one fact and another begins to bring the overall interpretation of a chart or table together.

By being used consistently such questions provide a clear and memorable way in which children can gradually approach charts and diagrams.

Why you need to know these facts

- The distinction between fiction and non-fiction needs to be established in the early stages of children's encounters with books. This should not just be a sense that different books take up different spaces in a library. Children need to develop an understanding of the different purposes of texts and the different ways in which readers read them. There is a tendency to provide children with a good grounding in fiction to the neglect of non-fiction. However, children need early introductions to the uses of non-fiction texts and the various features that guide the reader through their use, particularly features such as the contents page and the index.

- Evaluation of non-fiction texts should draw heavily upon the features of the text. Whereas with fiction teachers often know the name of a good author or develop their own personal list of favourite books, non-fiction titles are often only brought into the classroom to support a particular project. As such there is a need for some criteria to apply when selecting titles to form part of a project set or non-fiction collection. Faced with a choice of books on the same subject, the deciding factors could be the effectiveness with which the features listed above are deployed. For example:

– Do the chapter headings guide the reader through the overall subject?
– Are sub-headings relevant or are they just used to break up text?
– Are charts and diagrams clear and relevant or do they just glitz up a drab page?

● Through understanding how the features of non-fiction texts work, children develop their ability to work with such material. As they begin to use indexes and consult diagrams they break out of a linear mode of reading, in which the reader progresses page by page through a text, and start to key into the actual part of the book they need for conducting an aspect of research.

● Children also need to develop their skills of evaluating the effectiveness with which a text carries out a particular purpose. They need to be aware of the fact that, if they are finding a non-fiction text of limited help, the problem may lie with the text itself. As the children start to compare the ways in which different texts present the same information and begin to judge the effectiveness of a text's presentation of information, they are developing their independence as critical readers.

● Textbooks form a significant part of the material children will use as they progress through their education. The ability to comprehend the features of a non-fiction text's layout prepares children for the use of textbooks in maths, science and other subjects. Skills such as the awareness of how to interpret material set aside in separate boxes or how to locate a particular section, provide a grounding in the accessing of information within a text.

Binary key – a chart that subdivides categories using a tree structure in which categories branch into sub-categories.
Glossary – a section of a non-fiction text that lists and defines technical or specialist terminology.
Route diagram – a chart that connects various pieces of information in a sequence.
Spidergram – a chart that elaborates the various pieces of information stemming from a subject.
Sub-headings – headings used to subdivide information in a non-fiction text.
Typography – the print or 'type' style on a page, such as bold or italic lettering or the font used.

Vocabulary

● Conduct a fact-chasing exercise. Provide the children with a list of words and ask them to use non-fiction books to find out one fact about each word. The children should be encouraged to use contents pages or indexes to access the information.

● Ask the children to look at a contents page and consider what they would expect to encounter within each chapter. This will hone the children's skills of knowing where to look for a particular piece of information. It can also demonstrate to the children the unhelpful nature of some chapter headings. A book with chapters such as *Chapter 1* and *Chapter 2* doesn't exactly guide the reader to its subject matter.

● Alphabetical ordering skills provide a basis for accessing information in indexes and glossaries. Such skills can be reinforced through a range of alphabetical order games. For example, stick a word onto the back of each child. Tell the children that they have to put themselves in alphabetical order. They are not to read any label aloud but they can tell one person where they should be in the line in relation to someone else (for example 'You should be in front of her'). The line needs to be made without each child knowing what word they are displaying.

● Give the children old copies of the Yellow Pages and a list of companies and what they do. Ask the children to find the telephone number for each company. Choose the companies such that the children encounter the classic Yellow Pages problem of looking for something under the wrong headings, for example camcorders are not listed under 'c' but under 'a' for audio-visual – of course!

Register

Every act of communication has a register. To understand this concept, look at these sentences:

First take a medium sized...

The south facing... enjoys a commanding view over the...

He gazed into her...

Failure to appear at the specified... would necessitate...

Got to be going now, see you at the...

Although important content words are missing, a reader will easily detect the types of text these sentences come from. The vocabulary hints at the content. 'First take a... ' quickly places the reader in the context of an instructional text – we know this is unlikely to be a love story.

Register isn't just a matter of vocabulary. There are conventions that underpin certain uses of language. The terminology used, the way the sentences are constructed and the level of formality are all features that give a piece of text or speech a register. In her book *Genres in the Classroom* (UKRA) Alison Littlefair defined the elements that create the register of a communication as:

● the content: what the exchange is about. In linguistics this is sometimes called the field
● the means of communication, also called the mode
● the relationship between the speaker or writer and the audience to whom the communication is addressed, sometimes called the tenor.

Littlefair presents a helpful diagram of these three aspects of register:

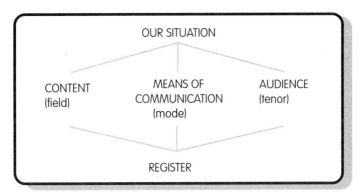

The conventions of these elements lead a writer to use particular vocabulary and style when writing; the reader then tunes in to these elements. These features create the conventional social routine for exchanges, so the formal letter to the bank manager will be couched differently from the note stuck on the fridge to a partner after a domestic bust-up. The field, mode and tenor guide the language user in the selection of words and the way in which they are used.

The registers of language used in non-fiction texts can result in the information they contain being couched in particular ways. Writers, including Bobbie Neate and Katherine Perera, have shown certain ways in which non-fiction texts adopt certain formalities of style and vocabulary. These can be categorised under the headings: vocabulary, sentence structure, cohesion.

Vocabulary

Non-fiction texts use new and unfamiliar terminology. This is unavoidable – indeed part of the job of such texts is to make new vocabulary accessible. For example, a text on the constitution might include terms peculiar to certain rituals such as 'black rod' and 'First Lord of the Treasury'. If such a text doesn't define the terms in the process of using them then it will alienate a number of readers.

In an article in *Language in school and community* (Edward Arnold, ed. Mercer), Katherine Perera points out the further pitfall of familiar terms being used in unfamiliar ways. She gives the example of words like 'caravan' and 'roads' which, in a sentence like, 'The camel caravans trudged the old silk roads between the ancient cities of Constantinople and Peking' take on a less familiar meaning to the usual one. So, as well as introducing new words, such texts can introduce new uses of familiar words.

Sentence structure

Non-fiction texts can present their readers with sentences that contain an unfamiliar sentence structure. In narrative texts sentences usually present events in a sequential order, written in the past tense. While there are non-fiction texts that will retell events in such a way, such texts can also present their material in the present tense:

The Upanishads is a special Hindu book.

Young Muslims learn large sections of the Qu'ran.

Such a use of the present tense is one example of the varied grammatical structures found in non-fiction. Perera defines these grammatical features as: 'sentence patterns less frequent in speech than writing'. It is the case that such texts will often structure their sentences in ways a speaker is less likely to communicate. She gives the example of altered word order, quoting the sentence:

They wanted to keep their gods happy. This they did by offering them gifts.

The second sentence is linked smoothly to the first, but a speaker is more likely to say: 'They did this...' Such unfamiliar word patterns can slow readers down.

Cohesion

The links across a text, one sentence linking with another to develop an idea, is called cohesion. Cohesive ties enable the reader to see how one sentence leads to another and to keep track of what a text is saying. These can be pronouns – as in this sentence in which the word 'these' refers the reader back to the term 'cohesive ties'. Also, connecting words like the one that started this sentence can perform the same function. Such ties provide what Littlefair calls 'the *thread* of meaning'. If they are not clear, the reader will 'lose the thread'.

There are two main forms of cohesion – lexical and grammatical. Lexical cohesion is established by similar words linking sentences across paragraphs. The previous two sentences share the word *lexical* linking the sentences and guiding the reader through the development of this subject. In grammatical cohesion, this is accomplished by grammatical features, including pronouns such as *this*, *it*, and *he*. For example, 'The Prime Minister entered the Commons. He was met by loud jeering.' Here, *The Prime Minister* is synonymous with *He* and this links the sentences.

In the preceding paragraph the words, 'In grammatical cohesion, this...' included lexical ('grammatical cohesion') and grammatical ('this' – synonymous with 'linking the sentences') examples.

In *Finding out about Finding out* (see Resources on page 82), Bobbie Neate points out that in some non-fiction texts the lack of connecting words can be confusing. She quotes the work of Pearson who compared sentences such as:

The peasants revolted because the king raised taxes.

Here the connection between the revolt and the rise in taxes is defined. However, without 'because', the connection becomes implied only:

The king raised taxes. The peasants revolted.

Pearson found that children preferred to work with sentences that guided by using such connecting words.

Reading non-fiction

Why you need to
know these facts

● Children should be introduced to a broad range of texts.
The texts that are included in home corners and structured
play areas in the classroom are an important part in this.
Texts in a play area should include actual, real-life texts,
such as brochures in the travel agents or a price list and
menus in the cafe.

● The conventions used in texts need to be imparted to the
children through modelling the reading process. The way in
which conventions place the reader in a particular role,
giving some hold on how the text is to be read and used, is a
key concept that needs to be highlighted wherever possible.
Letters home, instructions for making something and
information texts all place the reader in a particular role
and make particular demands that need to be discussed
with the children as the text is read. When encountering
these texts, understanding the new vocabulary will be only
a quarter of the activity. The discussion and action that
follow should be seen as part of the whole literacy process.
The following list shows texts children can look at as part of
their literacy development:

*advertisements, badges, CD covers, comics, directions,
e-mails, forms, graffiti, greeting cards, labels, leaflets,
letters, lists, magazines, maps, menus, newspapers, notes,
notices, plaques, postcards, posters, product packaging,
reference books, registers, shop signs, signs, stories,
tattoos, teletext, web pages.*

● Recognising that a text will do a particular job is vital to
children's ability to grasp how different texts should be
understood. There is a risk that children get an idea that the
sole purpose of the texts they encounter is to practise
reading the words on the page. Questions such as *What is
this text going to tell us?* or *What is the purpose of this text?*
bring home the idea that texts do something.

● Vocabulary plays an important part in any reader's
understanding of a chunk of non-fiction. A high priority
should be given to collating new words and keeping their
definitions in a way that children will find accessible,
whether on a chart or in a class dictionary. Attention should
also be paid to the varying uses of familiar terminology.
New uses for words should also be pointed out and defined
against the conventional usage. The main message here for
children is 'don't panic' – they can be thrown into a

submissive mode by an overwhelming level of unfamiliar words in a text. When encountering a difficult text, encourage the children to carefully unpick new definitions and to calmly reread the text.

● Re-reading and comprehending involves unpicking some of the unfamiliar sentence structures that children will encounter. Activities that involve rephrasing the content of sentences will help here. The following section on comprehension examines this.

● For the teacher, the above might also bring home the need to shorten the amount of material being studied. One paragraph of non-fiction, clearly researched and with the sentences interpreted and vocabulary understood, provides a far better text to share than endless pages that swamp a reader. Of course there are masses of texts that children will plough through as part of their own research work. But they will do this better for having had a shorter and more intensive time spent revisiting a passage of non-fiction in a way that gathers their attention, understanding and, most significantly, confidence with such texts.

Vocabulary

Field – the content and purpose of an act of communication.
Grammatical cohesion – links across a text established by grammatical words, such as *it, this* or *he.*
Lexical cohesion – links across a text established by vocabulary.
Mode – the means of communication, for example letter, e-mail.
Register – conventions that underpin certain uses of language.
Tenor – relationship between participants in an act of communication, for example teacher–child, bank manager–customer.

Common misconceptions

It is important to avoid the confusion that texts adopt a particular register and stick with it. A non-fiction text may move from an informal, anecdotal style into a formal detailed exposition. Many non-fiction texts for young children start with narrative openings, for example 'Sue and Sam are going to the farm'. The text might then shift into the factual information that was the agenda of the text all along, for example 'Farmer Spoggs explained how intensive, genetic modification of battery hens can increase yields'.

Reading non-fiction

● Look out for the fullest range of text-based opportunities from the children's own lives. The party needs some sort of plan for who will bring what food, the outing can have a map, the assembly a running order, the hamster cage its instructions for feeding and cleaning. There are very few things we do in life that don't have some text written about them. As teachers we sometimes mediate these to our class, reading the idea and then explaining it. It does no harm to give children access to the notes, task boards and plans that inform our teaching but it does widen the range of texts they encounter.

● Collecting texts is an essential part of teaching literacy. Keeping a collection of texts should be approached with the aim of finding the best examples for the widest range of text types. If, for example, a collection is to include headlines or newspaper articles, then these should be chosen selectively. Any newspaper would provide a load of articles but a useful collection will include the few that will really grab the attention of the children. I have had my newspaper story from *The Times* about the badger who crept into the washing machine of a rural householder and went through the full wash cycle, unharmed, for years. It still gets trotted out when my class look at news stories and is still a success.
    There are certain types of text that children can be encouraged to collect and features they can review within them. These include:
– Instructions: How easy are they to follow? What steps do they outline to do a particular task? Do they say too much or too little?
– Chocolate bar wrappers: How do they describe the chocolate inside? What other information do they give? What do the names tell you about the chocolate inside? Can you find bar wrappers beginning with each of the letters of the alphabet?
– Newspaper cartoons: Who is in the cartoon? What features are used to identify the characters? If it is based on a news story, which one is it? What joke does the cartoon make?

● Purposes to writing should be presented up front before a task is undertaken. Children should be encouraged to always have in mind who the audience will be and what the writing aims to do. This should be a part of the planning process. One quick activity is to spread a range of collected texts across a table, including chocolate bar wrappers, cereal boxes, adverts from newspapers, leaflets, letters and

postcards. Ask the children to work in twos looking at the
text concerned and making a note of its purpose. Ways of
unpicking this include asking:
– What does this text do?
– What would be missing if this paper was blank?
– What might someone do after looking at this text?

● Vocabulary needs to be kept accessible and comprehensible
as children tackle new subject matter. This could involve
the production of charts on particular subjects or word
books that keep a list of new words. A loose-leaf file with a
page devoted to each new topic will suffice for the latter. It
is worth being thoughtful about whether to include
definitions with such collections, as children can become
'hung up' on the one most visible on the chart or in the
word book. It is sometimes better to include the word as a
reminder of its place within a subject and allow children to
form their own definition over time, through reading.

Comprehension

Subject facts

The common image of comprehension is of a text followed
by ten questions. The text is unconnected to anything else
the child is studying and the questions must be answered in
sentences. The process is laborious. Such exercises train
children to match questions to bits of text and often don't
engage with any understanding of the text. In *Literacy and
Language in the Primary Years* (Routledge), David Wray and
Jane Medwell give an example of a text that reads:

> *The chanks vos blunging frewlwy bedeng the brudegan.
> Some chanks vos unred but the other chanks vos
> unredder. They vos all polket and rather chiglop so they
> did not mekle the spuler. A few were unstametick.*

The text makes no sense but the reader could still attempt
the following comprehension questions: 'What were the
chanks doing?', 'How well did they blunge?' and 'Where
were they blunging?'
   I recall encountering as a child a large box of reading
cards at school we were required to work through,
answering the questions. It soon became apparent to us that
we could answer the questions without reading the passage.
You just needed to match the key word in the question to a

bit of the passage and create a tidy answer. You could bluff your way through not having read the text. While it may have been excellent training for coping with the amount of DfEE papers that appear in school it didn't exactly promote my comprehension skills.

Comprehension involves reading a text and making a connection between the material encountered and prior knowledge – the things the reader already knows. To read: 'Thomas More was executed after a dispute with Henry VIII concerning the King's divorce' is to read a sentence that makes complete sense. However, its meaning misses readers who do not have some prior knowledge about Henry VIII or what is meant by 'the King's divorce'. It is for this reason that comprehension will always involve a dynamic process. The reader is never just taking in facts – the process is more of an engagement with text. The process can be described as follows:

- the reader knows something
- the reader anticipates the text's ability to add to this knowledge
- the text tells the reader more
- the reader adds this extra information to what is already known.

The reader is meshing one set of knowledge with a new set. Such a model places an emphasis on the prior knowledge and questions of the reader.

Frank Smith, in *Reading* (CUP), defined the process in dynamic terms, seeing the reader as always approaching the text with some idea of what it will say. Armed with this prediction the reader seeks answers from the text:

> *Prediction is asking questions – and comprehension is getting these questions answered.*

Skimming and scanning

Gathering information from a text often involves the skills of skimming and scanning. Skimming involves the reader moving his or her eye quickly across a text, taking in headings and noticing major subsections. Like the stone skimming over the water, the skimming reader flips through the pages or across the page, much in the way that many of us leaf through a daily paper to see what's covered where before knuckling down to individual stories.

Scanning homes in on particular details, picking out information on a particular topic and discarding the rest.

Like the reader who turns to the Used Car adverts in the paper with the specific intention of buying a Ford car, the scanner will home in on the word Ford and ignore other material roundabout.

In *Teaching Primary English: Teaching Reading at Key Stage 2* (Nelson Thornes) Nicholas Beilby provides a useful explanation of the two processes, drawing upon the way in which a dictionary is read:

> *When we are using a dictionary, we may well skim the page headers to locate the right page, but it is probably quicker, then, to scan the page, letting your eye seek your target word, rather than methodically working out where it is according to alphabetical order.*

Why you need to know these facts

● The texts used in class should, as far as is possible, possess a clear relevance to children. This may come through a connection between the text and a topic being covered in another curriculum subject. It can also come through using texts rooted in the popular culture with which children are in tune or through news stories that have a contemporary interest. The main aim is to begin with a text that children have a reason to read. As far as possible these should be complete texts, in the sense that they stand alone. A couple of paragraphs from a longer story can be very frustrating unless the fuller story is also encountered elsewhere.

● Comprehension requires demonstration. It is an excellent activity to undertake with a group of children as a way of sharing reading because this gives the teacher the opportunity to model the process. Faced with questions about a text, children need to work through an example with their teacher, seeing how the evidence of the text is turned into answers that connects with prior knowledge. With comprehension, a clear demonstration is essential to show how the various parts of the task fit into a workable process.

● Answering 'in your own words' requires some guidance. In particular children need some guidance on how to turn the evidence of the text into a worded answer of their own. Firstly they need to locate key terms in the part or parts of the text that deliver their answer. Then they need to construct their own sentence. This is the point at which they need to check that they have answered the questions.

This is a crucial point at which to reread the question, checking that the answer they are about to give addresses it directly. Children are often misled by questions and leap at a part of the text, giving what they think is the answer rather than the one actually required. The other reminder needed is that, as they formulate their 'own words' they need to be clear. They need to ensure their answer is a sentence that states the answer with clarity. They need to imagine they were reading that answer for the first time. Would it make sense to them?

● Skimming can begin from the early years, as children are faced with a text and draw on features they can perceive to suggest what the content might be. From that point onwards every opportunity should be taken to skim texts, otherwise children become hung up on reading the whole thing. Time is a useful tool here. Big books can be skimmed and discussed before they are read. As their reading progresses, children need to face a newspaper article with the instruction that they have half a minute to skim it. They need constant reminding that this does not mean reading from the beginning. Scanning can be reinforced by asking questions on a page that has not been read through in its entirety, asking children to locate the word that stands out as a key to the answer and work from that point within the text.

Vocabulary

Scanning – the location of particular words or features within a text.
Skimming – quick 'reading' of a text to locate main features, content and structure.

Teaching ideas

● Ask the children to devise questions about the text. This can be undertaken before they read the text as a way of anticipating the questions they expect it to answer. It can also be done as an activity for children who have read a text, devising questions for which it provides answers.

● Big book reading can lay the groundwork for skimming. Initial sight of a non-fiction text can involve skimming through – possibly raising questions about the subject of the book. (See also KWL grids on page 80.)

● Get the children to practise skimming during library

times as part of the process of selecting a book. Ask the children to look at the contents of a book and skim through it then report back to the rest of the class on what they have discovered about its content.

● Question slips create an interactive way of undertaking comprehension. In this activity slips with questions typed onto them are placed into non-fiction texts, acting as book marks for the page where children should begin their search for answers. A slip could be placed in the index, contents page or relevant section of the book. Information on the slip can guide children as far as is needed. For example, a question in the contents page such as 'What did a penny farthing cycle look like?' could add the signpost 'Look for a chapter with the word *bicycle*' giving the reader an idea how they can use that part of the book. The slips can show as much or as little support as is needed, geared to how accessible children will find the particular book.

● 'In your own words' activities give children an opportunity to phrase facts or ideas in a text in their own way. Give the children a passage such as 'An eclipse is caused when the Moon travels between the Sun and the Earth'. Get the children to try to find various ways or rephrasing that fact. They can be given the opening words for a rephrasing, such as 'If the Moon...' or 'An eclipse happens...' The introduction of new vocabulary (such as *If* and *happens*) gives them an idea of how new words enter 'in your own words' answers.

● Info-chasing. Giving the children a set of facts to be found within a pile of five or six different books. The fact should give a starting point for using the index or skimming through headings. Unfinished facts, such as:
– The telephone was invented in...
– The distance to the moon is...
– The capital of Kenya is...
make good starting points.
   Present the children with twice as many facts as books, with a fair spread of facts between the books on offer. Start the clock and the chase is on.

● Library research times can be adapted to take the format of popular quiz shows. In the past, teachers have drawn on 'Blankety-Blank' and 'Blockbusters'. Recently 'Who Wants to be a Millionaire' has provided a structure in which researchers climb a ladder of answers towards a million.

Researching and note-taking

Subject facts

Most readers approach non-fiction materials with a question or an idea about the subject they want to explore.

The process of researching and note-taking involves taking the information sought from texts and focusing upon what the reader wants. There is often another step of presenting that information, when chunks of information located in a range of texts are collated into a written report or verbal presentation on a subject.

Such a process often involves five stages:

- **Opening**   A question or subject. The basis of an enquiry.
- **Collecting**   Collecting material through note-taking or annotating texts.
- **Connecting**   Making links between collected material.
- **Synthesising** Scattered pieces of material are brought together in an organised way.
- **Using**   Presenting and using the information.

Opening

Opening an enquiry is the point at which the researcher has a question or subject that is the basis for the reading they will undertake. The more focused the question, the more precise the research process will be.

Brainstorming is one of the ways in which a subject can be opened for enquiry. A brainstorm is a chart on which the various features of a subject are branched outwards from the main heading:

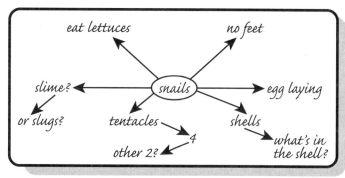

Collecting

Collecting involves working through a text or set of texts locating facts that meet the researcher's needs. This will often involve note-taking and the collection of material from a range of sources.

Note-taking

Note-taking involves collecting specific bits of information. Researchers don't write out entire texts. When making notes the most important pieces of information are taken down and other words in the text discarded. A useful starting point to understanding note-taking is to begin by looking at the difference between content words and function words. A sentence such as:

The electricity that we use comes from a power station.

contains certain words that refer to things or actions (electricity, generated, power station). These are content words, described by Alison Sealey in *Learning about Language* (OUP) as 'words which can be made to stand for the idea of some aspect of our experience of the world'.

Function words, such as *is* and *by*, link the content together. Their job is to structure and organise the sentences that communicate the content. Sealey points out that the first category, content words, will continue to grow. New words added to the language, such as *laser* and *Internet*, expand this category whereas the functional category is relatively fixed.

In note-taking, the researcher homes in on the content words, making notes. For example:

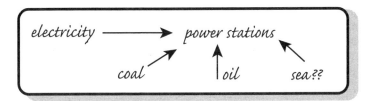

There are some ground rules that establish the difference between note-taking and structured, sentence-by-sentence prose:

● Information can be scattered on a page. Children can draw information maps in which information is taken down in a graphic way.

● The main pieces of information are all that is needed. This could involve listing the key words within a chunk of information.

● Researchers develop their own shorthand. Note how the notes on the planets below use a shorthand of a circle for moon – showing, for example 'Saturn has 23 moons'.

Good notes always keep a reference to source material. With this in place, ambiguities can always be rechecked. This example shown includes references to television programmes and books from which information was gathered.

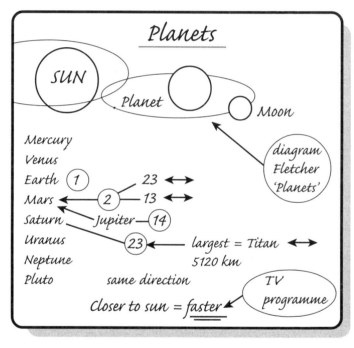

Annotating texts

Researching and note-taking usually involves gathering material from texts. It can also involve making notes on actual texts. To annotate a text is to mark it in a way that makes it more comprehensible to, and shows the thoughts of, the reader. Annotators will often develop their own shorthand for noting passages of particular significance or subdivisions within a text. Users of highlighter pens sometimes develop the most elaborate colour schemes for their annotation.

Connecting

Connecting involves making links between material collected from different sources. A reader looking for information on mosques will, by looking in a range of texts, find some facts emerging in more than one text, whilst some texts will be the sole source for a useful piece of information. Here, again, the use of a brainstorming chart can be useful. The chart used to open the subject can be added to with new information, establishing the connections within the subject matter.

Synthesising

Synthesising is an essential part of this process. Scattered pieces of material need to be brought together in an organised way. A piece of research into a locality picks up details about the history and geography of the place, the customs and current economic factors. Such information needs some clear synthesising, so that historical facts are gathered and sequenced, while geographical facts are organised in some way. What is crucial here is the grip the researcher now gains on the topic. It is as if other people's facts from other people's materials are now becoming the researcher's. The organising principles that enable this effectively synthesise what, until now, has been a scattered collection of materials.

Using information

The final stage in the process is using the information. The synthesised material is, at this stage, made into a presentable package. The reader will turn the material into a written report structured into paragraphs on different themes, a poster with various subsections or a lecture on the subject. It is at this point that the different ways in which information can be presented come into consideration. Charts, tables, comic strips, swingometers, fact cards – all are examples of the diverse ways in which information can be presented to an audience.

The main ways that the children will present their information gathered include:

- Written reports in which the text is structured into paragraphs.
- Word lists in which key words are presented with information.
- Bullet point fact sheets on which the main points are itemised.
- Diagrams that represent information graphically.

● Tables in which rows and columns interact to organise information.
● Flow charts in which connections explain points gathered around central subject headings.

● The way in which an inquiry or investigation into non-fiction opens proves to be a crucial part of the process. Children need to be taught to develop good questions or narrow enough lines of inquiry otherwise they are at a loss as to which book to open and for what purpose.

● Note-taking needs to be removed from the laborious attempt to rewrite information word for word. Children need to see how the filleting of information sources for the significant material can provide the researcher with a series of notes to replicate in a new form as a new text. The points listed on page 76 above can be taught in sessions in which children read and collect information in groups or as a whole class.

● Information needs to be represented in different forms. In gathering information children need to be aware of the ways in which they might eventually present it.

Vocabulary

Annotating – making marks on a text.
Synthesising – the organising of a set of facts in a systematic way.

Teaching ideas

● KWL grids were initially suggested by D M Ogle (in *Children's Comprehension of Text* ed K Denise Muth, 1989) and provide active ways in which children can develop a research process. The KWL system works around a simple table divided into three columns headed:

– What we <u>K</u>now
– What we <u>W</u>ant to find out
– What we have <u>L</u>earned/still need to learn.

Before looking up information on a topic, children complete the first column, noting what they already know about a topic. They may know that there are lots of planets.

The next column provides a space for children to anticipate what they may be able to find out. One child may say there are millions of planets, another that there are only seven. Once they have completed this second column children have laid the groundwork for some researching, guided by a sense of what they anticipate finding out.

The final column provides a space to make notes about what has been found out.

What we know	What we want to find out	What we learned
There are lots of planets	*How many planets are in our solar sytem?*	

● Questioning can be developed in a number of ways. Children need to gather a list of good questions that will spark off research into information texts. The use of the question starters: *who? what? when? where? why?* and *how?* can stimulate their creation of varied questions. After picking a subject they can try and think of a set of questions starting with different words from the list.

● Word rating is one way of developing note-taking skills. Read a passage of information to the children twice, the first time encouraging them just to listen carefully and the second time with the children noting down some of the words from the passage that they think are important. Be specific about how many words the children should note down.

Once they have listed their words, get the children to work in groups to compare the words noted down. They should look for words that everyone noted, words that only one or two people noted and so on. They can try splitting the words they noted into premier league, first division and second division words. The premier should contain a third of the total number of words on their list but be the ones that are most important. The other two divisions organise noted words by level of importance to the subject.

● Give the children a page of information text. Ask them to read the text and then to cross out words, phrases and sentences that are not vital to the subject matter. This way they focus on the main bits of a text that would be collected in note-taking.

● Practise annotation skills with the children. There are various ways in which a text can be marked and children could use the markings for different purposes, for example an underlined word could mean 'this is important' or 'this needs defining'. Some of the main marks that can be made are:
– underlining
– circling
– writing sub-headings in the margin
– highlighting in different colours
– numbering to show different sections.
Give the children a piece of text and ask them to circle words they need to look up, underline the main facts, highlight the sentences they think are the most important, write sub-headings to denote the main subject of each stanza and number the paragraphs to create a point-by-point breakdown.

Resources

Finding out about Finding out: A practical guide to children's information books, by Bobbie Neate (Infopress) A short and accessible book that takes the reader through the main areas of non-fiction. The books draws on Neate's research into a range of non-fiction texts and maintains an incisive sense of what books for children are actually like and how best to use them.

Extending Literacy: Children reading and writing non-fiction, by David Wray and Maureen Lewis (Routledge) A comprehensive book that covers the subject of non-fiction fully. The writers present many strategies for thinking and planning through this area, including a clear explanation of KWL grids. The model of non-fiction use they present is particularly useful.

Using libraries – the main resource
Many of the skills outlined in this section can be enhanced by ensuring children visit and use a library. Local library services are keen to develop such links. This is vital because:

- it develops both the skills and purpose that will be vital to a child's ongoing use of library services
- local libraries are often better able to provide a wider range of up-to-date information texts than a school can provide.

To make sure links are effective, the teacher needs to establish:

- the protocol for such visits: when and how often children can visit
- any routine that may involve children joining the library which will often require parental permission.

Above all, library trips should be purposeful. They should be underpinned by time spent in class looking at the subjects that will be researched, explaining any classification system the library may have and planning who will research what and when the visit takes place.

Build up a good relationship with staff at the library. They can be a vital lifeline for good, quality information gathering.

Chapter 4
Types of non-fiction

The one heading of non-fiction encompasses a wide range of text types. As with the genres of fiction, there are familial features that such texts share in common. An understanding of these features can enable a structuring of non-fiction writing.

Non-fiction genres

Subject facts

Different texts perform different purposes. A recipe has a different purpose to a film review – both will be read and used differently and the writing of both will be organised in different ways. Also, film reviews deal with different films and different recipes make different meals. However, film reviews all follow a similar pattern and different recipes share certain common features. Within this group of text types there are common elements. Recipes have similar structures although the end results can taste very different.

The texts within a genre may be structured in similar ways, have particular patterns in their writing and have similar language features. Texts giving instructions are likely to include verbs that instruct, for example 'Pour... Whisk...' However, a recount of the making of the same food would use different verb forms, 'I poured... I whisked...'

There is a vast array of non-fiction text types. This

chapter will focus on the six genres that serve common and widely used purposes:

- recount texts
- instruction texts
- report texts
- explanation texts
- persuasive texts
- discussion texts.

Each section will look at structural and language features in such texts. These features are summarised in the chart which can be found at the end of this chapter (on page 107). Remember that, in such texts, structure and language are guided by a clear purpose.

Why you need to know these facts

- An awareness of the variety of types of non-fiction will broaden the writing repertoire in the classroom. In the past, story-writing has often had an over-dominant role in shared writing. An understanding of the structure and language features of certain types of non-fiction text can provide teachers with a model to adopt in shared writing. This can then provide children with guidelines for their own writing.

- The twin perspectives of structure and language can provide a way of identifying the similarities that often emerge within a family of text types.

Vocabulary

Genre – a grouping of similar texts.
Language feature – particular aspects of the language of texts, such as common verb tenses or particular types of word usage.
Structure – how a text is organised; the relationship of the parts of a text.

Common misconceptions

It is important not to restrict the number of genres used in the classroom. In schools there is a tendency to focus on a set number as if they were the only ones. Teachers need to bear in mind that the use of language and evolution of texts is an ever-changing area and that, while this chapter outlines six particular examples, there are more. The six examples are a useful means of developing a range of writing strategies but should not become strait-jackets.

● Send the children out around the school to see how many different text types they can find. They will encounter warnings, instructions, texts telling readers how to use certain things, information on displays and so on. This activity can transfer over to homework – ask the children to list of some of the texts in use at home, for example shopping lists or television listings.

● Give the children a large collection of different text types including newspaper cuttings, menus, recipes, instructions and so on. Ask them to consider the job each one does. As they do this, encourage them to start to group the texts. For example you could ask them to separate the texts into piles of those that recount things that happened and those that don't. The children should also be encouraged to think about how each text has a purpose and that critical readers can discern that purpose.

● Give the children a variety of texts and ask them to pick out the similarities and differences between them. This works well if children are given a selection of texts that includes some texts from the same genre and some from others. For example, if the children are given a diary entry, an advert, two recipes and another piece of instruction text, such as the rules for a game, they will be able to find similar features as well as differences between the texts.

Recount texts

A recount text records a series of events. Chapter 3 looked at some of the structural features of narrative texts; some of these features can be found in most recount texts, however, the genre of recount is much broader than that of stories. Recount texts can include news stories, diary entries, historical records and retellings.

Structural features
Recount texts can vary in the way in which they present events. The following features provide a basic structure:

● **Orientation.** The opening of a recount text will often present the reader with some idea of the events that are about to be recounted. Journalism students are sometimes told that they should open their story with a single-sentence paragraph of 20 words answering the basic questions *who?*, *what?*, *when?*, *where?* and *why?* For example:

> *Brave Sam Parker from Carton, Berkshire yesterday received a special award from the pensioner whose life he had saved.*

This orientation gives the bare bones of what will follow. It opens the recount that will flesh out the details.

● **Events.** Recounts are largely tailored around a series of events, structured in chronological order. For example:

> *As Sam was riding home from school last Tuesday, he noticed the front door of Mrs Wilson's house was open. Sensing something was not right, Sam approached the house only to find that...*

However, as with fictional narrative, strict chronology can be broken by flashbacks of earlier events:

> *Sam knew what to do. Only last year he undertook a Home Safety Award at his primary school, achieving...*

Events can be recounted in a variety of ways. The recounting of events can include broad and sweeping statements:

> *Lenin returned from exile and started a revolution.*

or more specific detailed recollections:

> *Lenin looked out of the window and watched as they passed by the villages and farmyards.*

● **Conclusion.** At the end of the recount text, the events are usually summed up in some way. A diary entry might end:

> *All in all it was one of the worst days I have ever had.*

or a news story might conclude:

> *Mrs Wilson said, 'I will never be able to thank him enough.'*

There is often a 'rounding off' of the recounting of events.

Language features

● **Specific participants.** Recount texts involve specific participants. Unlike recipes, which might say, 'First you take an egg...' and refer to any 'you' taking any 'egg', recount texts will refer to specific people, places and things:

Ms Brown, the keeper, took the ostrich egg and...

● **Past tense.** Recount texts are usually recorded in the past tense. These texts usually retell something that has happened and therefore draw upon a verbal structure that matches the task:

Next day, the explorers hacked through the forest. That night they found a clearing and pitched their tents.

Why you need to know these facts

● While story-writing is one of the most common forms of language activity in the primary school, there is still a need for children to be taught how to structure a recount of events. Children will often deliver a list of facts in order about, for example, a historical event they have researched. These often need organising into a structured recount. Features like the orientation and the conclusion can provide a more rounded recount of events.

● The recounting of specific participants is a particular issue for teachers at Key Stage 1. Children will often recount an event in a way that can do with some elaboration, for example 'That's the man and he sees the boy' (Carter, aged 5). They should be encouraged to fill out more specific details about who the man is, which boy he sees and what the connection is between them. This provides an opportunity for work on proper nouns as opposed to common nouns and the use of capital letters.

● Well-structured recounts organise a succession of events effectively. One particular skill is representing historical events. This involves being able to elaborate on the range of minor happenings that made up an event like the Spanish Armada or the Fall of Benin. Children should be encouraged to try splitting events, providing more information on one event in their recount. If, for example, they end a piece of writing with: 'Guy Fawkes went to Parliament but got caught', they can pick this sort of statement apart to itemise some of the events involved in that one all-embracing sentence.

Chronological order – the order in time in which events occur.
Orientation – an opening section of a text giving some idea of the events to be presented in a recount.
Past tense – verb forms for events that have taken place, for example *ran, walked*.
Recount – a text that records a series of events.

Vocabulary

● Ask the children to produce a diary around a particular event. This could be a diary of their first week in a new class, a school trip or the preparations for an event in school. The diary could be in the form of a scrapbook with bus tickets, programmes, notes and other mememtos from the event. An activity like this provides a good focus for children who need to elaborate the details of a recount as it provides the teacher with an opportunity to pick out the smaller events that combined to make the larger event.

Teaching ideas

● Newspaper stories make an excellent resource for looking at the recounting of events. Having looked at the format of such stories, children can be encouraged to write their own, giving them a 'who, what, when, where, why' opening before proceeding to outline events and include quotes from witnesses and participants. Children can do this with a variety of raw material including:

– events they have experienced
– events recounted to them by adults
– events they have watched on a news programmes
– events they have looked at in history, for example a report on the Spanish Armada.

● When the children are preparing to recount an event, ask them to answer these five key questions:

– what happened before the event?
– what happened after the event?
– what did someone say during this event?
– what did someone think or feel during this event?
– what was really good or really bad about this event?

These questions should help them to fill out their account. For example, if they have written 'I went to the park with Tom', these questions can help them to dig deeper, avoiding a quick sense of 'I've finished'.

Instruction texts

Recipes, instructions on how to assemble something, rules for playing a game, doing a trick or delivering a particular classroom activity – all these are examples of instruction texts. Sometimes referred to as 'procedural' texts, they take the reader through a set of steps towards a particular goal, explaining 'how to' achieve it.

Structure

Instruction texts are usually structured around a series of steps which the reader will need to follow to perform a particular task.

● **A goal.** Instructional procedures will often begin with a statement of the goal that is to be accomplished. This can be an opening:

> *Here's how to make a stunning pop-up card for your friends or family.*

Texts of magic tricks sometimes open with an account of how the illusion will appear to an audience before explaining how to perform it. Recipes will often begin with a description of the dish to enthuse the reader.

● **Materials.** At the outset of a task, there is usually a list of the materials which will be needed to achieve the goal. For example:

> *You will need:*
> *sheet of card*
> *paper clip*
> *pipe cleaner*

● **Step-by-step directions.** Having given a list of what is needed the instructions then tell the reader what to do. These commands are systematic, sometimes in a numbered or bulleted sequence. The main structural point here is a step-by-step progression, isolating and ordering the specific steps in a procedure, for example:

> *1. Fold the card in half.*
> *2. Place the clip on the middle of the fold.*

Such steps are often supported by figures or diagrams.

● **Hints.** Within such texts small hints can be given. These can include warnings, such as:

> *Boiling sugar can be very hot. Make sure you have an adult helping you.*

or tips for the job, such as:

> *Leave the potatoes to go cold before coating them with the melted butter.*

● **A conclusion.** The procedure can close with a direction as to how the thing made can be used or some other comment that rounds off the instructions, such as:

> *Once you have made this pop-up you could try using the same idea to make other animal cards.*

Language features
● **Imperative verbs.** Instruction texts are usually written with imperative verbs, issuing commands. These are often placed at the beginning of sentences, for example '*Fold* the card in half. *Place* the clip on the middle of the fold.'

● **Simple present tense** verbs. Directions can be given in a simple present tense form, such as 'First you *cut* the paper, then you *fold* the paper.'

● **Second person.** If participants are mentioned, it is usually in a second person form, for example 'First *you cut* the card. Then *you fold* the paper.' The participants are impersonal, leaving the text open to whoever might read and undertake the activity.

● **Connecting words.** Where connecting words are used they will signal the step-by-step process involved in the activity, for example '*First* cut the card. *Then* fold the paper.' This connection can be indicated by a numbered or bulleted sequence.

● **Prepositions.** Instruction texts will often contain a number of prepositions. These will provide detailed direction as to where or when a procedure is to take place, for example 'Cut the card *between* the folds. Glue the tab *under* the flap. Fold the tab *into* the other side.'

Types of non-fiction

• If children understand how instruction texts are structured, they will be able to access them more effectively. This is a crucial skill for children as it enables them to use textbooks and instructions more independently.

• The activity of writing instructions gives children a particularly clear sense of their audience. Children can produce instruction texts with a clear idea of the effect of their writing. When writing recounts children often miss out important details such as where or when something took place. When writing instruction texts they can see how every detail counts. There is a twin-track approach to this writing, in which they are marrying their text with their clear idea of what they want the reader to do.

• Instruction texts can be of particular use in technology. As children complete designing and making tasks they can use their growing understanding of this genre to outline the steps taken in their work.

Vocabulary

Hints – small pieces of information or advice within an instruction text.

Imperative verbs – words that command the reader to do something, for example *Boil a kettle, Cut the paper*.

Instruction texts – texts outlining a set of steps towards a particular goal.

Prepositions – words that indicate where or when something is in relation to something else, for example *under, on, before*.

Procedural texts – a term sometimes used for instruction texts.

Simple present tense – the simple present form of a verb, for example *make, find* (often used as a heading for a verb, such as *to make, to find*).

Teaching ideas

• Give a group of children three or four books about how to do magic tricks. Ask them to look at the list of materials and decide how useful and complete the list is. How clear do they think the step-by-step instructions are? Did they find one book easier to follow than another? Can they say why that was?

• Ghastly or fantastic instructions provide a diverting variation of instruction texts. Spells and recipes from writers such as JK Rowling and Roald Dahl serve as good starting points. Ask the children to produce their own fantastic spells, revolting recipes or weird instructions, such as how to make a magic potion or how to escape from school. Explain to the children that they must follow the correct structure and language for instruction texts.

● Divide the class into pairs and give each pair a selection of wooden blocks, boxes of different colours, cotton reels, kitchen-roll inner tubes and plastic bottles. Ask each child to construct, unseen by their partner, some sort of arrangement using the objects. Then ask the children to write instructions on how to make their construction. Can the child's partner follow the instructions to produce the same arrangement?

This activity could be varied by asking the children write directions to a location within the school or instructions to create a 2D abstract drawing.

Report texts

Report texts present information on a subject. They organise information in a way that paints a picture in words for the reader. Unlike chronological writing they just state what something is, what it is like or what it consists of. For example:

Subject facts

wasp: *a wasp is a winged insect. It has a sting and is characterised by the thin stalk between the head and the thorax.*

Structure
Report texts are non-chronological in that they do not follow a passage of time in what they present. They don't tell a story about their subject, they just present it. There is a basic structure that can underpin such texts.

● **General presentation.** A report will often open with a general idea of the subject matter. A piece of report writing describing a location may open with a general description of the location, such as:

Graves Park Animal Farm provides home to some of the rarest breeds of farm animals in the country.

● **Moving to the particular.** One of the most important structural features in a report text is the way in which the text starts with general introductory material and then moves to discuss specific details about the subject. The main body of this section of the report text will be descriptive material. However, this is not the poetic description of literary texts – the descriptions tend to be specific and analytical, for example:

> *The caterpillar breathes through air holes which can be found on the side of its body.*

● **Final summary.** Report texts will often be wound up by a final summary, leaving the reader with a final concluding point about the subject:

> *This variety of interesting nooks, crannies, shops and cafes makes Robin Hood's Bay a fascinating village.*

Language features

● **Present tense.** Report texts will use 'timeless' present tense verbs. The texts might report that a river '*runs* through the town' or that an animal '*lives* in a shell'.

● **Generalised participants.** Report texts involve generalised participants. Rather than a particular caterpillar they refer to 'caterpillars'.

● **Linking verbs** play an important part in report texts. Verbs such as *is* and *has* link one aspect of the subject to another, so 'the caterpillar *has* air holes' or the 'snail *is* a gastropod'. Such verbs show the relational links between the details of the overall subject.

● **Objective tone.** Reports retain a formal and objective tone. They tend to give facts about a subject. They avoid the inclusion of overt opinion.

Why you need to know these facts

● Children find it hard to put chronological narration 'on hold'. When asked to write about something, such as a description of their school, they will often naturally incline to a story about children in the school or a recount of their journey to school. The idea that writing can flesh out the details of something is one they need to practise if they are to develop the distinctive qualities of this genre. The impersonal, objective tone needs to be reinforced.

● Report writing can provide good links to subjects such as Geography and RE where children can often be asked to recount the details of a particular place or belief.

Generalised participants – general categories such as 'the frog' rather than specific characters such as 'Kermit the Frog'.
Non-chronological – not structured according to the passage of time.
Report texts – texts that present information on a subject, creating 'a picture in words'.
'Timeless' present tense – the present tense of the verb, as in what the subject does at present, for example 'the caterpillar *lives*, 'it *breathes*'.

● Writing sentences about a photograph or postcard provides a good starting point for younger children to begin describing the main picture and then develop sentences of smaller observations in report format.

● Ask the children to write a report on a local area, such as the layout of the school or the local community. Encourage them to subdivide their planning for writing into separate sections, each reporting on different parts of a location. Encourage them to see the text as a map in words that gives the reader some image of what they would encounter if they walked through the location.

● Objects can provide a good basis for the early stages of report writing. The use of words like *is* and *has* can be promoted, making simple structures such as, 'The wall is crumbly. It has green slime on it.'

● Get the children to write a report of an animal without including its actual name. Ask them to read their text to the rest of their group. Can their group guess what animal they have reported on? Make sure that the guessing side listen to the whole text before having a guess – texts that begin 'This animal has a trunk at the front' can be short-lived otherwise.

● Invented subject matter can provide an opportunity to practise this type of writing without getting too hung up on the content. Inventing a minibeast, new school or a holiday resort can provide a basis for devising a report.

Explanation texts

Explanation texts, like report texts, provide information. The difference is that, whereas report texts present non-chronological information about a subject, explanation texts outline a process. Explanation texts take a particular phenomenon and explain how or why it occurs. For example, this explanation takes us through the Earth's water cycle:

The water cycle takes the Earth's water through various steps. Water is lost from the Earth's surface to the atmosphere by evaporation caused by the Sun's heat on the surface of lakes, rivers and oceans. The water turns into vapour and then rises upwards. This atmospheric water is carried by the air moving across the Earth. It then condenses as the air cools and forms clouds, which in turn deposit moisture on the land and sea as rain or snow. The water that collects on land flows to the ocean in streams and rivers.

It could be said that if a report text is like a picture, an explanation text is like a flow diagram.

Structure

In an explanation text, the *process* is the crucial element. Such texts tend to quickly move from a brief orientation to the presentation of the process they are explaining giving the two-part structure of:

● **Presentation of the subject.** Explanation texts open with an indication of the process they are going to explain. An explanation of rainbows will open with a statement about the phenomena such as:

If the sun shines during a shower of rain this sometimes causes a rainbow to appear in the sky.

● **Step-by-step process.** Having presented the subject, explanation texts will then describe the way in which such a phenomena occurs. This will usually follow a series of generalised events. For example:

The sun shines through the raindrops. The raindrops refract the light from the sun.

There is a step-by-step sequence to the process as one thing causes another and, in this way, the text shows how a particular thing happens.

Language features
● **Temporal connectives.** Explanation texts are often moved along by temporal connectives. These are connecting words and phrases that show the link between one thing and another in time. For example:

> *The water evaporates* when *the sun shines* then *forms vapour.* **After** *that it rises upwards.*

● **Causal connectives** also play an important part in such texts. These are connectives that show the cause and effect relationship between things. For example:

> *The water evaporates* because *the sun shines. It turns to vapour and* **consequently**, *rises upwards.*

● **Simple present tense verbs,** such as *turns* and *evaporates* denote the actions in such texts. The text isn't describing a process that happened once or that took place in the past but a process that happens repeatedly.

● Chronology is a key feature of explanatory writing. Once children have grasped the idea of following a process in writing, they make a marked improvement in their writing of this genre. Often, having been asked to explain how something happened, such as how a balloon was made to fly around the room, they will focus on writing one part of the process, such as where it landed or how it looked as it moved. The essential element here is the step-by-step process.

Why you need to know these facts

● Causal links provide the structure needed throughout the writing of such texts. Children need to develop the skill of turning their observations into explanations. After observing and learning about a process they need to make the connections that become an explanation. Having experienced the process of inflating a balloon and letting go, children need to unpick the causal links that made one thing lead to another. As such this genre of writing has particular links to children's work in science.

● The beginnings and endings of explanations need some

attention. Children will often explain a process but leave out the start or the end. Taking the balloon example again, they will begin an explanation with the words 'When the balloon is full of air' without stating how the balloon came to be full in the first place. Sometimes such details are unnecessary but, as a rule, children need to be encouraged to check the fringes of their explanatory process to make sure they have tied up loose ends.

Vocabulary

Causal connectives – connecting words and phrases that show how one thing caused or was caused by another thing.
Explanation texts – texts that outline a process, explaining how or why something happens.
Generalised events – events that happen again and again (for example, rockets taking off) rather than at one particular moment in history (for example, Apollo 10 taking off).
Temporal connectives – connecting words that link things in time, for example *then*, *later*, and *after this*.

Common misconceptions

One text can contain more than one genre. A leaflet on a power station can move from being a report-type guide, to an explanation of how the power station works, to a procedural text instructing the reader how to make their way around the building and ending in reportage outlining how the power station was built. Within any particular text there can be a range of genres doing a variety of jobs.

Teaching ideas

● Get the children to use a series of A6 boxes to plot a process they are trying to explain. Ask the children to explain how the water cycle, or another suitable process, operates using a series of loose A6 boxes. Ask them to write each different stage of the process in a separate box. Once you have checked their work, they can put any missed steps in a new box, which can be inserted in the correct place. Once a full set of boxes thoroughly outlines the process, the children can stick these down to complete their text.

● To develop the children's understanding of the elements of explanatory texts, use some simple, visual processes that children can explain, such as:
– what happens when an inflated balloon is released
– how a candle reacts when the flame is lit
– the effect of a stone thrown into a pond.

● Give each child in a group of six a part of a process, such as the digestion process, either to remember or to write on a piece of card. Ask the group to organise themselves into a line that represents the correct order that food is eaten and digested. Ask them to read out their various parts of the process and ask the rest of the class to consider how clear the wording is or whether alternative phrasing would improve the text.

Persuasive texts

Persuasive texts proffer an opinion and aim to win the reader around to their viewpoint, for example political rhetoric, letters in the local paper or petitions to people in authority. The texts are structured in a way that hammers home a particular point of view.

Subject facts

Structure
In short, the structure of a persuasive text is one-sided. It keeps a hold on a particular argument, clearly stating an opening view, reasons for the argument, the opposing view and a conclusion.

● **Views**. The opening statement will often be the viewpoint to which the text is drawing its readers. Persuasive texts have a case to be made. This can be explicitly stated in the opening. There are persuasive texts that hide this clear statement of the subject until later, preferring to reason an argument through to such a point as an inevitable conclusion.

● **Reasons**. Persuasive texts will proceed to outline the reasons for the initial argument. These can be stated and supported by other information.

● **Points on opposing views.** At some point in a persuasive text, opposing views will be stated. These are usually put up only to be knocked back down again, such as:

There are those who claim hunting keeps down the number of foxes but this fails to account for the cruelty of blood sports.

● **Concluding statement of the argument.** Having hammered home its points, a persuasive text usually returns to the original argument to put it once again. This can be in the form of a direct appeal to the reader, for example 'Stop these cruel sports'.

Language features

● **Connectives.** Reason-orientated connectives such as *therefore* or *for this reason* will be more common than those that are time-orientated, such as *before, later, after all this*. Unlike chronological texts in which the connectives structure events, the connectives in persuasive texts link causes and effects:

Fox hunting is wrong because it causes distress to foxes.

If you smoke, then you will damage your health.

● **Timeless present tense.** In persuasive texts, sentences often use the timeless present tense: 'Foxes *attack* farm animals', 'fox hunts *damage* the countryside'.

● **Judgmental.** Vocabulary often includes language that express an opinion on something, for example *good*, *unwholesome* or *ridiculous*.

● **Modal verbs** are used to express the surety of certain statements: 'Fox hunts *could* be banned', 'Fox hunts *should* be banned', 'Fox hunts *must* be banned', 'Fox hunts *will* be banned'.

Why you need to know these facts

● Children need to be made aware of the difference between facts and opinions. As an initial step in the understanding of this type of writing, children need to be aware of the issues and subjects that can be treated in a persuasive manner. They will be used to being bombarded by the persuasive power of advertising, however, they will need to be introduced to the idea of adopting a stance on an issue as an aspect of citizenship and social education. The most effective way of doing this is by looking at current local or national issues such as fox hunting and look at the opinions that can be held on these. Encourage children to talk to adults at home as part of the formulation of their own viewpoints.

● In learning how to make a persuasive case children need to be aware of the different levels of moderation in which this can be done. Advertising can be one extreme of the spectrum, and Chapter 7 on Media texts (see pages 140 to

152) will return to the razzmatazz that often goes hand-in-hand with this type of persuasive text.

● Controlling the persuasion is an important aspect of this learning process. It is no good saying 'Mr Smith is wrong because he is a silly old berk' – yet there is a tendency in children learning the process of persuasion to resort, through frustration (or enjoyment), to such means. The essential element here is to tell children not to be insulting but to persuade by the reasoning of their argument. As they read or watch pieces of persuasion in local papers or on panel discussions children need to be alerted to the twin features of views and reasons. They need to look out for a view being supported by reasons. This structural feature is integral to their understanding and use of this type of writing.

● Unpicking viewpoints is another skill that underpins this type of writing. When they are arguing a point children need to be encouraged to try and find as many reasons as they can to support the argument. They will often resort to one reason for their opinion and stick to it. Careful planning of persuasive writing should involve elaborating an argument by giving a range of reasons in support of that point of view.

Modal verbs – verbs that express the likelihood or certainty of other verbs. If, for example, someone says 'I make boats' then there is no doubting the statement. Modal verbs, such as *could* or *will* express how certain an action is, for example 'I *could* make boats', 'I *will* make boats'.
Persuasive texts – texts that aim to influence the reader towards a particular opinion.

Vocabulary

Remember that the genre titles given above are only convenient labels for types of text. They enable us, as teachers, to explore the particularities of a type of writing and, most importantly, offer guidance to our pupils in writing in a range of genres. It must be remembered that there is no clear dividing line between them and that elements cross over between texts. A report text could be said to 'explain' information just as persuasive text could be said to 'explain' a particular opinion, but in this chapter we have referred to 'explanatory' texts with a particular, narrow definition.

Common misconceptions

● As a class, read or watch a news item, possibly drawing on a programme such as *Newsround*. After the item has been read or shown, ask the children to come up with an opinion about it. Help them to realise that there are issues over which people adopt an opinion.

● Try to find a subject on which the whole class is likely to have the same viewpoint, such as whether the school field should be ploughed up to build a new shopping centre or whether playtimes should be shorter. On issues such as these it should be likely that everyone will be of one mind! Ask children to work in small groups to come up with reasons to support that opinion. Gather these together on the board, noting any that are made by two separate groups, then ask the children to gather these points together in a persuasive piece of writing.

● Have a good argument. It is a vital way of developing the children's persuasive skills. This involves being awkward and giving the other side of an issue with a view towards children having to sharpen their reasoning to counter you. Use a subject, as above, on which the children all have the same viewpoint about. Argue against them, for example, that the area needs a new shopping centre on the school field. This will push the children to see the opposing views for which they must account. In time the children themselves can try doing this, looking at the argument they are making with a view towards seeing holes in their viewpoint and considering if they would be swayed by the persuasive points being made.

● Newspapers can provide interesting examples of persuasive material. As a class, look at an editorial from a tabloid paper that hammers home a particular case. Look also at the letters page which will often include responses to issues arising in the area with an opinion and the points to support it.

● As a class, watch an extract from a panel programme in which different people put across different points of view. Show the children a snippet in which a question is asked and two panellists give their opinions. At this point, stop the tape and ask children what they picked up from the snippet. Stress that anything they understood is valid. They may not understand the details of the two sides but they will often pick up on the fact that the two people disagree, how angry they are, whether one says the other has lied and so on. Encourage them to look for the opinions stated and the supporting reasons given. Obviously, when undertaking such a task the subject matter of the disagreement is vital. Children will gather more from a fall out over fox hunting than inflation.

Discussion texts

Discussion texts explore the various positions that can be taken up on an issue. They can express two sides of an argument or explore the various positions around a contentious matter.

Subject facts

Structure
Discussion texts can structure themselves around the number of viewpoints they present. To retain an element of balance they need to give a fair footing to the two sides of an argument. Balance is achieved in a structure that includes:

● **Statement of the issue under discussion.** The issue can be introduced with an indication of what it is, why it is contentious and why it is relevant, for example:

> *Britain's membership of a single currency is an issue that raises high passions concerning sovereignty and financial control and yet one on which the country will soon have to reach a decision.*

● **The presentation of one point of view.** In discussion texts, first one point of view will be aired, with an indication of what that standpoint happens to be and the reasons why some would adopt it, for example:

> *Some would argue that staying out of a single currency will isolate Britain from the rest of Europe.*

● **The presentation of an alternative point of view.** The first airing of a standpoint will then be balanced by an alternative viewpoint, for example:

> *The alternative view is that Britain should retain control of its own finances.*

Such an alternative can act as a rider to the initial point of view, for example:

Though in response to this it could be argued that control is no use if you're too isolated to make the most of it.

This might then be followed to a return to the original point of view, followed by a return to the contrary point of view. Such texts can keep putting the initial and contrary points of view across. The text can revisit the sides of the argument, allowing each to counter the other.

● **A summation on the subject.** Discussion texts will sometimes conclude with a summation. This can sum up the pros and cons of the different sides in the argument or reach an opinion based on the arguments put by each side.

Language features

● **Modal verbs** will be used to show the conditional nature of some of the assertions being made in a discussion text. These are verbs that qualify a main verb so, instead of saying 'Trains run on time', modal verb like *should*, *might* or *don't* is used to show the conditionality of what is being said:

Britain **should** *join the single currency.*

● The vocabulary used will include adjectives that pass a judgement. Words such as *good, bad, excellent* and *unwise* will express a viewpoint on an opinion or statement, for example:

Trains should run on time. This is **unlikely**.

Why you need to know these facts

● The ability to see two sides of an issue involves a mature ability to adopt a distance from the sides of an argument. Children need to be able to present contradictory viewpoints and to elaborate the different sides in a discussion. Children should learn to present a viewpoint they do not necessarily hold, getting inside the reasoning involved in that argument.

● Discussion texts play a significant role across the curriculum. They can provide a way of presenting some of the features of history that children study. They can also feature in discussions that take place as part of PSHE as well as in considering issues of citizenship, including learning to respect for the opinions of others. The ability to present the ideas of differing viewpoints is also an essential part of religious education. As children progress through their education, discussion texts will also feature in the geography and economics work.

Discussion texts – texts that explore the various positions that can be taken up on an issue.
Modal verbs – verbs that qualify a main verb, for example *should, might* or *don't*.

Vocabulary

Persuasion and discussion are often mixed up. In persuasive texts one point is being made and, while this may involve mentioning the opposing view, this is usually done with a view towards undermining it. Persuasion is about convincing the reader that an opinion is right. Discussion texts involve a more open presentation of the differing opinions on an issue, with a view that the reader should not have one final point pushed upon them.

Common misconceptions

● Ask the children to write a statement such as 'Children should walk to school if possible' at the top of a page and to divide the page into two columns underneath the statement. Tell the children to present arguments for and against that statement in the two columns. Supply suggestions to any side that is flagging.

Teaching ideas

Children should walk to school if possible	
For	Against
Keeps you fit	Roads are dangerous
Cars ruin the environment	It rains
Walking is more interesting	You'll get tired

● Get the children to work in teams of two on a selected issue and to write a few sentences each, each taking a contrary side on the issue. Once they have done this independently they can then share the two sides and use them as the basis for writing a short discussion text.

● Take an issue, such as excessive car use or fox hunting and get the children to ask as many adults as they can, at home and at school, to give an opinion on it. Back at school, write the issue on a large sheet of paper at the front of the class and note around it the views the children have gathered. This information can then be used as a basis for a discussion text. To be really wide-ranging, children could e-mail their MP or telephone a local interest group and ask for a viewpoint.

Resources

Exploring How Texts Work, by Beverly Derewianka (Primary English Teaching Association, Australia)
Exploring the Writing of Genres, by Beverly Derewianka (United Kingdom Reading Association)
These two texts by Beverly Derewianka provide the most accessible introductions to the work of the Australian genre theorists. The former is fuller but much harder to obtain. The latter presents a brief and useful guide to the main text types.

First Steps: Information Texts, Key Stage 2, by R Bindon (Ginn Heinemann)
A practical book, outlining a range of non-fiction genres and giving clear planning materials for teaching the range in the classroom.

Developing children's non-fiction writing, by Maureen Lewis and David Wray (Scholastic)
This book provides an excellent presentation of the features of various genres. It also offers suggested ways of framing texts to help children write in the various genres.

Non-fiction texts: a working guide

Recount texts	Instruction texts	Report texts	Explanation texts	Persuasive texts	Discussion texts
STRUCTURE					
orientation	a goal	general presentation	present the subject	an opening view	a statement of the issue under discussion
events	materials	particular	step-by-step process	reasons for	the presentation of one point of view
conclusion	step-by-step directions	summary		points on opposing views	the presentation of an alternative point of view
language features	hints			concluding statement	a return to the contrary point of view
	conclusion				a summation on the subject
LANGUAGE FEATURES					
specific participants	imperative verbs	present tense	temporal connectives	connectives that reason	modal verbs
past tense	simple present tense	generalised participants	causal connectives	modal verbs	adjectives that pass a judgement
	step-by-step connecting words	linking verbs		judgmental vocabulary	
	prepositions giving where or when directions	formal and objective tone		timeless present tense	

Chapter 5

Poetry

The teaching of poetry should never be mired in subject detail. Poetry is supposed to take language and bring it to life – not deaden all pleasure. However, subject knowledge does have a place in enhancing the appreciation of particular forms of poetry and exploring various styles. Building from the very sounds of poetry, there are features of the text and language that can support teaching.

Phonetics

Subject facts

Rhyme

Roses are red
violets are blue;
some poems rhyme
but this one doesn't
Anon

The distinctive feature of much poetry is the use of the sounds, or phonetics, of the words. The commonest perception of poetry is that a poem is a set of sentences that rhyme. While this tells only a small part of what poetry is and does, there is nonetheless a strong tradition of the use of rhyme in poetry. Certainly, nursery and playground rhymes, the first poems that children encounter, rhyme.

A rhyme is created by the sound, or phonetics, of two words. When two words end in a chunk that sounds alike, they rhyme. These words may also have similar spelling patterns, such as *night* and *sight*, or they may have different patterns, such as *night* and *site*.

A number of simple poems create impact by combining rhyme with a pattern of similar line length. For example, Janet and Allan Ahlberg's:

> *Each peach, pear, plum*
> *I Spy Tom Thumb*

Here, both lines are created from four monosyllabic words and both lines end with the sound *–um*.

Rhymes can be full rhymes, half rhymes or internal rhymes.

● **Full rhyme.** In the example above, *plum/thumb* is a full rhyme.

● **Half rhyme.** A half rhyme occurs when two words almost rhyme, but don't quite. They may have similar consonants and similar, but not the same, vowel sounds. In 'A Bird Came Down the Walk', Emily Dickinson approaches a bird on the path:

> *Like one in danger, Cautious,*
> *I offer him a Crumb*
> *And he unrolled his feathers*
> *And rowed him softer home*

Crumb and *home* don't fully rhyme, but create a half rhyme: *-mb* and *-me* sound the same, but *-u-* and *-o-* only sound similar. Half rhymes are a feature used to full effect by Emily Dickinson in many of her poems.

● **Internal rhyme.** Internal rhyme occurs when two words rhyme within the same line of poetry. In 'He Wishes for the Cloths of Heaven', WB Yeats describes 'heaven's embroidered cloths' as:

> *The blue and the dim and the dark cloths*
> *Of night and light and the half-light,*

The repetition of sound *–ight* in the second line – *night, light* and *light* – is an internal rhyme.

Rhyming patterns

The patterns of rhyming lines can vary from poem to poem. In Helen Russell's poem 'My Shadow', pairs of lines rhyme:

> *As I walk home to have my tea,*
> *My shadow skips along with me,*
> *When I skip, then he skips too,*
> *He copies everything I do.*

When, as in the above example, two lines of poetry rhyme side by side, the pairs of rhyming lines are called rhyming couplets.

A different pattern can be seen in Rossetti's 'The House of Cards', where the second and fourth lines rhyme:

> *A house of cards*
> *Is neat and small:*
> *Shake the table,*
> *It must fall.*

The arrangement of rhyming lines can be shown by marking the opening line of a poem with an **A**. Each line that rhymes with this line is then also marked as **A**. The next unmarked line can be marked with a **B**, along with the lines that rhyme with it.

Using this scheme the Helen Russell poem shows an AABB pattern:

> *As I walk home to have my tea,* **A**
> *My shadow skips along with me,* **A**
> *When I skip, then he skips too,* **B**
> *He copies everything I do.* **B**

The rhyme in Rossetti's 'The House of Cards' follows an ABCB pattern:

> *A house of cards* **A**
> *Is neat and small:* **B**
> *Shake the table,* **C**
> *It must fall.* **B**

The Clerihew

The Clerihew is a type of rhyming poem in which two rhyming couplets provide a potted biography of an individual. They are named after their inventor, Edmund Clerihew Bentley (1875-1956), who composed examples such as:

Daniel Defoe
Lived a long time ago.
He had nothing to do so
He wrote Robinson Crusoe

and

What I like about Clive
Is that he is no longer alive.
There is a great deal to be said
For being dead.

Alliteration

When words in close proximity start with the same
consonant group, they are said to alliterate. For example,
from 'Freedom' by Mary Dawson:

I am going where the <u>gr</u>een <u>gr</u>ass <u>gr</u>ows
And fields <u>fl</u>aunt their wild <u>fl</u>owers;
Where <u>sw</u>allows <u>sw</u>oop and skim under the sallows.

The repeated *gr-* sound in the first line, along with the *fl-*
and *sw-* of the following two lines are an effective use of
alliteration.

Assonance

Assonance occurs when words with similar vowel sounds
crop up within a few lines. For example, in 'He wishes for
the clothes of Heaven', by WB Yeats, there is a repetition of a
long *ee* sound:

I, being poor, have only my dr<u>ea</u>ms;
I have spread my dr<u>ea</u>ms under your f<u>ee</u>t;

● As children develop their critical appreciation of poetry,
they will begin to recognise not just that some poems rhyme
but also the ways in which rhyme works within poetry. In
the early years, this can take the form of children creating
rhymes of their own – this activity often accompanies their
developing awareness of the sounds in words.

● Research has shown that sensitivity to rhyme can play an
important part in reading development. Learning that
similar sounding words sometimes look similar can support
children's development as readers and writers. Children
who hear the similarities between *Jill* and *hill* can also

Why you need to
know these facts

identify the similar spellings in such words. If they then confront an unfamiliar word like *fill* their previous understanding of this spelling sequence will help them to decode the new word.

● An awareness of phonetics can enhance a reader's enjoyment of poetry and is an important element of a child's ability to read poetry aloud effectively.

● Children should be encouraged to produce rhyming poetry for themselves. While the use of rhyme can be restrictive and ought not to be imposed on all poetry activities, it is nevertheless a tool the poet can use for effect.

Vocabulary

Alliteration – the repetition of a consonant sound.
Assonance – the repetition of a vowel sound.
Clerihew – a short summation of a person in two rhyming couplets.
Couplets – two rhyming lines next to each other.
Phonetics – the sounds of human speech.
Rhyme – the effect created when the endings of words sound alike, for example *cat/hat*.

Amazing facts

Clerihew Bentley is said to have invented the 'Clerihew' during a boring chemistry lesson.

Common misconceptions

Many children – and many adults – use rhyme as the defining factor in deciding whether a piece of language is a poem or not. While rhyme can create a special quality within a poem, it isn't an essential feature – many great poets, for example Dylan Thomas and TS Eliot, rarely if ever used rhyme.

Teaching ideas

● Create a rhyming dictionary as a class. This can be produced as a book or chart on the classroom wall, with various words organised according to their rhyming chunk. For example, the *all* page will include *call*, *fall* and *tall*. Encourage the children to use the rhyming dictionary when writing rhyming verse or song lyrics.

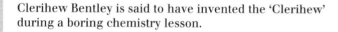

• Rhyming games provide a good foundation for this area of poetry. Younger children can try to think of words that rhyme with an initial one-word stimulus suggested by the teacher.

• Get the children to produce their own versions of shorter published poems. For example the children could create their own versions of Michael Rosen's 'Down behind the dustbin' poems:

> *Down behind the dustbin*
> *I met a dog called Jim*
> *He didn't know me*
> *and I didn't know him*

Children can produce their own example using their own name or that of a friend. For example:

> *Down behind the dustbin*
> *I met a dog called Sean*
> *He said 'Have you seen my mate?*
> *I don't know where he's gorn!'*

Another adaptable idea can be found in Pauline Clark's poem 'My Name Is...':

> *My name is Sluggery Wuggery*
> *My name is Worms-for-tea*
> *My name is Swallow-the-table-leg*
> *My name is Drink-the-sea.*

By matching and rhyming a set of nonsense names children can create their own poem following this pattern.

• Give each child in the class a different letter of the alphabet and challenge them to create an alliterative line of verse using their letter. Display the lines as an alliterative alphabet. It could begin with:

> *An amazing, ample, apple*
> *Some beautiful, big, blue balloons...*

• As a class, create pairs of rhyming couplets. This activity always primes a class of children to make a rhyme. Children are happy to play along with a task that is only two lines long. Teachers then find it surprising when the class keeps on devising.

Rhythm and language

Subject facts

Poetic language involves a careful relationship between the lines of a text. This relationship can be one of rhyme or rhythm. Within the lines of poetry the language can be structured to create a particular rhythm. Look at some famous lines such as:

I wandered lonely as a cloud

Twas brillig and the slithey toves

Do not go gentle into that good night

There is something in the pattern of sound in these lines that leads the reader to express the line in a particular way. This property of poetry is at its most evident when the length of the lines are considered. Many texts do what the lines on this page tend to do – start at one side of the page and go to a new line when the other edge of the page has been reached. Poetry doesn't tend to do this. The end of a line is an element of the structure of the poem rather than the practicalities of the page.

Metre
Lines of poetry often possess a distinctive rhythm. This is called its metre. For example, the nursery rhyme 'There was a crooked man' has a definite beat to it, and when it is said aloud, there are strong and weak beats in each line that are emphasised to different degrees:

x / x / x /
There was a crooked man

x / x / x /
He walked a crooked mile

x / x / x / x
He found a golden sixpence

x / x / x /
Upon a crooked stile.

Here, the metre has been mapped out and marked above the lines of verse. Where there is a strong beat – where emphasis is placed on certain syllables when the line is read aloud – the syllable has been marked with a forward slash /, traditionally referred to as the ictus. The weaker beats, traditionally called the remiss, have been marked with an **x**. A pair comprising an ictus and a remiss is called a metrical foot. In the rhyme of 'There was a crooked man', the metrical feet make up a 'de-dum, de-dum, de-dum' pattern as it is read aloud.

In some poems, the emphasis placed on the syllables is reversed, with a stronger syllable being followed by a weaker one:

> /   x   /   x   /   x   /
> *Jack and Jill went up the hill*

Here we have a 'dum-de, dum-de, dum-de' pattern.

A metrical foot with a 'de-dum' (x /) pattern is called an iamb and is a common form in poetry. A metrical foot with a 'dum-de' (/ x) pattern is known as a trochee. Poetry that follows a rhythm comprising iambs is said to be iambic. So, an iambic tetrameter is a line of poetry with four metrical feet (the tetrameter), each foot being an iamb. For example, from 'Jabberwocky' by Lewis Carroll:

> x   /   x /   x   /   x   /
> *Twas brill-* | *-ig and* | *the slith-* | *-ey toves* |

> x   /   x /   x /   x   /
> *Did gyre* | *and gim-* | *-ble in* | *the wabe...*|

Alternatively, Shelley's poem 'Ozymnadias', while having an iambic pattern has lines with five feet. This is known as the iambic pentameter:

> x / x /   x   /   x /   x   /
> *I met* | *a tra-* | *-veller from* | *an an-* | *-tique land* |

> x   /   x /   x   /   x   /   x   /
> *Who said:* | *Two vast* | *and trunk-* | *-less legs* | *of stone...*|

As you say these lines aloud, you hear the emphasis falling on words like *said*, *vast* and *stone*. This is the iambic pentameter at work. Iambic pentameter is a common form of verse in the work of Shakespeare:

> x   /   x   /   x   /   x /   x   /
> *But, soft!* | *what light* | *through yon-* | *-der win-* | *-dow breaks?*

Poems can vary between iambic and trochaic emphases:

/   x   /   x
Hump-ty | Dump-ty

/   x   x   /
Sat on | a wall

The rhythm here shifts from 'dum-de, dum-de' for 'Humpty Dumpty' to 'dum-de, de-dum' for 'Sat on a wall'.

Stanzas

Poems can be structured into verses or stanzas. The stanzas are the equivalent of paragraphs in prose and are separated from each other with a line break. A stanza maybe as short as two lines or substantially longer. A poem can have many stanzas or just one.

The arrangement of stanzas will often form a pattern throughout a poem – each stanza may contain the same number of lines and might follow a pattern of rhyme or rhythm. In 'My Shadow', by Helen Russell, the lines quoted on page 110 form one stanza. The next two stanzas are also four lines in length so that the pattern of the first stanza returns again and again, giving the poem a repeated rhythm and rhyme pattern.

In song lyrics, many of which have crept into poetry anthologies, the stanzas will sometimes be interspersed by a repeated chorus. This device is also used in some poems. For example, in 'The Jumblies', by Edward Lear, each stanza ends with the repeated chorus:

> *Far and few, far and few,*
> *Are the lands where the Jumblies live;*
> *Their heads are green, and their hands are blue,*
> *And they went to sea in a Sieve.*

Rap

Rap poetry developed from within the reggae tradition of Jamaica. In rap poetry words are accompanied by a strong beat of bass and drum, accompanying the voice delivering tightly packed lines drawing on the richness of strong dialect. For example, 'Write-A-Rap Rap', by Tony Mitton:

> *Hey, everybody, let's write a rap.*
> *First there's a rhythm you'll need to clap.*
> *Keep that rhythm and stay in time,*
> *'cause a rap needs a rhythm and a good strong rhyme.*

Haikus and cinquains

Haikus and cinquains are particular styles of poem that
have clearly defined characteristics in the way the syllables
and lines are structured.

- *A haiku* is a three-line poem with a distinctive
17-syllable arrangement of five-seven-five: a line of five
syllables, a line of seven syllables and another line of five.

    It can best be defined and demonstrated by the following
example by Eric Finney:

> *Haiku*
> *Poem in three lines:*
> *Five syllables, then seven,*
> *Five again; no rhyme*

- *The cinquain* is five-line, 22-syllable poem with the
syllables arranged in a two-four-six-eight–two sequence, as
demonstrated in this example by Gerard Benson:

> *Cinquain*
> *A short verse form*
> *Of counted syllables...*
> *And first devised by Adelaide*
> *Crapsey*

Free verse

While the use of rhyme and rhythm is a resource upon
which poets can draw, the tradition of poetry has roamed
free of seeing these as restrictive and required. There is
also a strong tradition of free verse, in which poets
construct their lines without subjecting them to a metrical
or rhyming structure. Often the lines will vary in length. In
free verse the endings and beginnings of lines are organised
to lead the reader to read them in a particular way. For
example:

> *In free verse*
> *the endings and beginnings of lines*
> *are organised*
> *to lead the reader to read them*
> *in a particular*
> *way.*

The reader is guided by line endings to pause in certain
places emphasising certain lines. This can be seen used to
its fullest effect by Michael Rosen in his poem 'Babysitter':

You go to bed before we
go out
AND
YOU
STAY
THERE.
"OK," I said, "OK OK OK,"
and off I went to bed.
I lay there waiting to hear the front door close.
SLAM.
and straightaway
I was
outthebed
downthestairs
intomybrother'sroom.

Dialect poetry

Dialect poetry is increasingly and rightly taking its place
within the mainstream of material in circulation. To
achieve the effective representation of the dialect in which
the poem is produced, the poet may vary the spelling and
grammar. This gives the poems a character that is seen in
Valerie Bloom's transcription of children anticipating the
arrival of their Headmaster in the poem 'Tables':

Ah wonda who tell all o' yuh
Sey dat dis class-room is a zoo?
Si-down, Head-master comin' through de door!
"Two ones are two, two twos are four".

Narrative poetry

Various styles of poetry can be used to tell a story. Narrative
poetry is, as its title suggests, the use of poetry to convey a
storyline. This can be as simple as the exploits of Jack and
Jill or as ambiguous as the mysterious traveller in
Longfellow's 'The Tide Rises, the Tide Falls':

The tide rises, the tide falls,
The twilight darkens, the curlew calls;
Along the sea-sands damp and brown
The traveller hastens toward the town,
*   And the tide rises, the tide falls.*

This poem, like many other narrative poems, sets out a
series of narrative events but leaves the reader to guess at
the gaps behind the story. This is also true for 'The
Listeners' by Walter de la Mare:

'Is there anybody there?' said the Traveller,
Knocking on the moonlit door;
And his horse in the silence champed the grasses
Of the forest's ferny floor.
And a bird flew up out of the turret,
Above the Traveller's head:
And he smote upon the door again a second time;
'Is there anybody there?' he said.

The reader knows that the traveller has arrived and that no one opens the door to him, but there is so much more that the poem does not say. Why does the traveller come to the town? Where does he go afterwards? Why does the traveller knock on the door? Who was he expecting?

Why you need to know these facts

● An understanding of metrical structure can enhance children's reading of the lines of poems. This is not to say that children will run a quick metrical check on a poem before reading it. However, the knowledge that poems can be structured in this way can affect the way in which children both read poems to themselves and perform them aloud. The importance of rhythm to rap performance is just one example of such structures at work in the way in which readers engage with poems. The terminology is not vital. A 'trochaic tetrameter' may sound daunting. Remember we are talking about the beat in poetry. Younger children may best be left with that term. Older children may enjoy a term like 'iambic pentameter'. It certainly gives them a good answer to the legendary inquiry, 'What did you do at school today?'

● Focusing on stanzas can provide children with a structure they can latch onto as they pick a poem apart. Children can take each stanza and grasp what is happening within it, before putting their grasp of these individual units together.

● Through forms such as cinquains and haikus, children can discover the way in which poetry, though short in words, is long in development. One of the frustrations teachers experience as they develop poetry writing with children is the speed with which children trot out a set of lines without taking in the structure of the poem. Through writing haikus and cinquains, children can be encouraged to 'write less, try more' – the short poem should be produced through a process of experimenting with various drafts and collecting various words that could be used.

● Children can enjoy the freedom of writing free verse, but should also experiment with how the line structure and line length can influence the way the lines are read. The idea that interesting and engaging free verse can be harder to produce than rhyming lines is one children need to be reminded of as they enter into such activities.

Vocabulary

Chorus – repeated lines between the verses of a song or poem.

Cinquain – a poem consisting of five lines with the syllable structure two–four–six–eight–two.

Dialect – a distinctive variety of grammar and vocabulary, often connected to a particular region.

Free verse – poetry free from restrictions of rhyme and metre.

Haiku – a poem consisting of three lines with the syllable structure five–seven–five.

Metre – the rhythm created by the syllable structure of lines of poetry.

Narrative poetry – a storyline told in a poem.

Pentameter – a line of poetry with five metrical feet.

Rap – poetry from within the reggae tradition of Jamaica with a strong rhythm.

Tetrameter – a line of poetry with four metrical feet.

Verse – a group of lines forming a section of a poem.

Amazing facts

● Tetrameter and pentameter might sound familiar to children. They will have encountered the Greek root word for four and five – tetra and penta – in maths. A tetrahedon has four faces; a pentagon has five sides.

● The iambic pattern is similar to the rhythm of a human heartbeat. It isn't regular and clock-like, but speeds up and slows down, always following that 'de-dum, de-dum, de-dum' pattern. Children can try listening to their own heartbeat – like poetry within.

Teaching ideas

● Children can appreciate the way in which syllables create a metrical structure in poems by clapping along with syllables in the rhymes they learn. As children develop their grasp of this structural device they can be encouraged to adopt a quieter method, such as closing their fists, saying a line and extending a finger for each line they say.

● Regular lines, such as pentameter lines can be used as a model for children to try creating their own ten-syllable lines. They can try saying these with the same rhythm used in poetry adopting this form. This can then be extended into creating iambic couplets, in which children devise one line to rhyme with another. So they could devise a simple statement in iambic pentameter:

x / x / x / x / x /
I am not sure if this line fits its feet.

They could add another line:

x   / x / x   / x / x /
I've tried to shape my words to fit the beat.

● As a class, write a dramatic sentence that can be used as the basis for free verse. If the poem is about their city, get the class to talk through features of the city until they come up with a notable line that has potential to be worked upon in various ways, such as 'In the evening there is a red sun over the tower blocks'. Write the line on the board and then get the children, in twos, to organise the sentence into two or three lines. Encourage them to say each version aloud to see how the line endings create different emphases in different places. For example:

In the evening
there is
a red sun over the tower blocks.

In the evening there is
a red sun
over
the tower blocks.

They can try various versions, noting down their two favourite arrangements. There is the potential for them to try this with three or four other lines, building up a poetic word picture in free verse.

● Haikus and cinquains provide obvious potential for children to try their own variations upon a theme. Children can also try developing their own forms. Ask them to devise the three-line poem with a pattern of two–four–six syllables or one–three–five syllables. They could follow the child whose train poem:

train
speeding
down the railway line

follows a distinctively train-like syllable count.

● Encourage the children to look at song lyrics as examples of poetry. It is with good reason that the song lyrics of Bob Marley, John Lennon and others can today be found in anthologies of great poetry. Contemporary lyrics for the children to study can be found in magazines, for example *Smash Hits*, and on the Internet.

● Narrative poems can be turned into storyboards. Ask the children to imagine they are filming the narrative and need to decide on a set of scenes that will be filmed as part of this. Plans for these can be drawn onto a series of rectangles that can then be stuck down onto a larger sheet, showing how the film of the story will unfold. The detail could range from three pictures to plan out 'Jack and Jill' to the detail of a storyboard of 'The Listeners' that includes a close-up of the traveller's face and his hand knocking upon the door. Children can write lines from the poem underneath each rectangle to record what stage in the poem is being filmed.

Imagery

Subject facts

Figurative language involves the use of words to create a striking image. It moves beyond the conventional use of words and is sometimes referred to as semantic deviation. (Semantics is the linguistic term for the ways in which words have a conventional meaning.) For example, there is a conventional understanding of the word *night*. However, when Dylan Thomas implores his dying father with the moving words:

Do not go gentle into that good night

he is using the word *night* in a different way. Night is presented as a place his father is travelling to, symbolising an ending. There is also a play upon the parting *goodnight* and an association with falling asleep. Thomas could have used plain words and said: 'Don't die quietly' but instead he uses powerful words loaded with a fuller potential and open to interpretation. The deviation in meaning pushes the reader to see familiar things in a different way.

Similes

Similes are one way in which this deviation can be done. A simile is a comparison between the attributes of the subject and an otherwise dissimilar object, for example 'as slow as a tortoise', 'as thick as thieves' or 'as smooth as a baby's bum'. Direct links are made through the words 'like' or 'as' between the subject and the object that also possesses the quality.

When the narrator in 'Daffodils' by William Wordsworth decribes himself as wanding as 'lonely as a cloud', he is not suggesting he turned big and fluffy and wafted around the lakeland skies! It is a deviation from the literal and conventional and it becomes one of the most famous and striking images in the English canon. Arun Kolatkar, in his poem 'The Butterfly', uses a simile to describe a butterfly:

> *It is split like a second*

The likeness provides a rich image and has the effect of stopping the reader, causing us to think more and deploy our imaginations.

Metaphors

Metaphors are another way in which language is used to create an image. In metaphors the direct link of *as* and *like* are taken away and, instead, the words just create an image of one thing in language normally reserved for another. In 'Poetry Jump Up', James Berry uses a carnival as a metaphor for poetry:

> *Tell me if ah seeing right*
> *Take a look down de street*
>
> *Words dancin*
> *Words dancin...*
> *words wild and free*
> *joinin de poetry revelry*
> *words back to back*
> *words belly to belly*

The poem describes a carnival scene in which words are dancing in the street. Language normally used to describe one thing, a carnival, is being used to describe another, a poem.

Concrete poetry

Concrete poetry uses the way the poem looks on the page to create an image. For example 'Friendly Warning' by Robert Froman uses the height of the words to depict the fate of the grass, moving from long to cropped words. Shape poems use words to create a shape important to the subject of the poem, so Steve Smith's poem, 'If the Earth', speaks of attitudes to the planet in a poem forming the earth-like shape of a circle.

● Imagery needs to be introduced to children as something to enjoy. For both children and adult readers the imaginative use of language in a poem can cause a distancing from what the poem is saying. Unless readers are taught to enjoy this effect they can become impatient with it.

● Looking for images is one of the ways in which children can develop their exploration of poetry. However, children can be very literal – they will tend to think Wordsworth is dressed up in cotton wool and floating around in the sky. So, when working on a poem with a group of children the teacher needs to be mindful of all the deviations in the language.

● Part of a sensitivity to imagery will be implicit in the way in which images are explored with children. You can't just brief them with a quick breakdown along the lines of 'Now these words are not really dancing – that is a metaphor'. In teaching about a poem, imagery can be explored through questioning that opens out the image. This can involve two avenues of exploration:

– The image itself can be explored. Children can be asked to delve deeper into an image asking what they think of when they imagine a street carnival or how a cloud looks as it goes through the sky. They need encouragement to explore the feelings conjured up by the image, such as the excitement of the carnival or how it would feel to move like a cloud.
– The subject or idea represented by the image can be explored in ways that ask 'in what way is x like y?' So children can be asked in what ways they think someone's wanderings could be cloud-like or in what ways the words of a poem are like people at a carnival.

Note: It is important not to deaden an image by explaining it. Questioning and discussion may result in a diverse, out-of-control set of interpretations – but that's why the image is so powerful!

● In their own creative writing, children can use similes and metaphors to create images.

Vocabulary

Concrete poetry – poetry in which words are shaped to create a visual image linked to the poem.
Figurative language – the use of words to create a striking image.
Metaphors – the creation of an image of one thing in language normally reserved for another.
Semantic deviation – language deviating from conventional meaning.
Simile – a comparison of two things using words such as *as* or *like*.

Common misconceptions

Similes and metaphors are often confused. The distinction is between a quality, such as 'sweet' being directly likened to something else, 'sweet like chocolate' in a simile and the likeness being implicit in the way in which something is described in a metaphor. In Berry's 'Poetry Jump Up' there isn't a simile along the lines of 'words **as** exciting **as** a carnival' or 'words scattered **like** dancers'. The metaphor paints the fantastic picture of words dancing.

Teaching ideas

● Comparison charts can be used to explore similes and metaphors with the children. Take, for example, 'He Wishes for the Cloths of Heaven', by WB Yeats. In the poem, Yeats describes his dreams as being like a carpet on which someone can walk:

I, being poor, have only my dreams;
I have spread my dreams under your feet;
Tread softly because you tread on my dreams.

Divide a sheet of paper into two columns and use the two things likened in the metaphor – the dreams and the carpet – as the headings of the two columns.
Next, ask the children to think of something about one of the things listed at the top of one of the columns and record their thoughts in that column, for example they might write

'You put these out for special people' under 'carpet'. Then ask them to draw an arrow to the other side of the page and, in that column, record why the first thought may link to the heading of the second column. The chart might look like this:

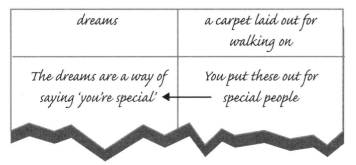

dreams	a carpet laid out for walking on
The dreams are a way of saying 'you're special' ←	You put these out for special people

Through making comparisons such as these children explore and extend the image beyond the boundaries the poet might have intended.

● A simple way into exploring imagery with young children is to create some similes. Give the children a tray of objects that look and feel differently. Get them to take turns to pick one object and say what it is like. They may decide that a key is *old*. They then need to think of something else that is *old* to make the simile link, such as 'as old as the school' or 'as old as a Granny'.

● Create a simile web with the children. Choose as a subject something that the children are familiar with and which can be described in various ways, for example 'rain' or 'a cat'. Ask the children to write this word at the centre of a sheet of paper. Then ask them to write around the subject four words that could describe it. For example:

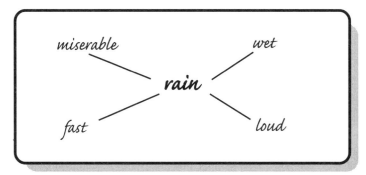

Ask the children to pick one of the describing words and to think of four things that also possess this quality:

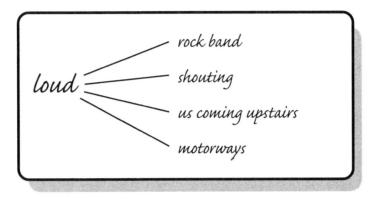

These webs can be used to create similes, such as 'rain as loud as shouting', 'rain's noise like a rock band' or 'rain as loud as a class running upstairs'.

● Metaphors can be explored as disguises. Give each child a slip of paper on which is written the name of an object or a feeling. Tell them that they have to write four metaphors for their word. If, for example, they are given 'fear' as a subject they can write about something that they imagine to look or feel like fear – responses can be as varied as a boiling kettle or a full moon. Remind them that when they write their metaphor, they need to recall the original impetus. Once the children have written them, ask volunteers to read out their metaphors. Can the rest of the class guess what the original subject was?

● Get the children to write shape poems. Remind the children that they need to make their lines scan so that the reader reads the poem in a particular way. It isn't enough to just draw a picture using any old word about the subject. The length of lines has to be governed by the metre. The shape is an added challenge.

● Letter poems cause children to give attention to a concrete shape while also thinking about the arrangement of words on the page. To produce these children write a poem in the shape of the initial letter of the poem's title. So a poem about home is written in the shape of an 'H' and a poem about the city in the shape of the 'C'. The simplicity and familiarity of the shape can help in the construction of the poem.

Resources

Poetry collections:

A Spider Bought a Bicycle and other poems, edited by Michael Rosen (Kingfisher)
Sit on the Roof and Holler, edited by A Rumble (Puffin)
Twinkle Twinkle Chocolate Bar, edited by John Foster (Oxford University Press)
Three excellent collections for younger children, with a range of poets represented in each volume. The sign of a good anthology is that it has a bit of daring, being prepared to include obvious material alongside the unexpected.

The Kingfisher Book of Children's Poetry, edited by Michael Rosen (Kingfisher)
The World of Children's Poetry edited by Michael Rosen (Kingfisher)
Together these two volumes encompass a diverse and lively array of poems. The material ranges from nonsense doggerel to poems like 'Ozymandias' and pieces of Chaucer. The two comprise a complete set with which to resource teaching.

They can be complemented by Kaye Webb's excellent *I Like This Poem* (Puffin).

Gerard Benson's *This Poem Doesn't Rhyme* provides a walk through various aspects of unrhymed poetry.

Every Poem Tells a Story, by R Wilson (Puffin), is a well-selected collection of narrative poetry.

Poetry Jump-Up, compiled by Grace Nichols (Puffin)
Can I Buy a Slice of Sky?, edited by Grace Nichols (Puffin)
Two collections of poetry from black writers, providing a rich collection of poems drawn from diverse cultures.

Individual poets

While the range is too great to include a full list of who's who in this area, here are some of the best titles from current children's poets.
Quick, Let's Get Out of Here, by Michael Rosen (Puffin)
Sky in the Pie, by Roger McGough (Puffin)

Talking Turkeys, by Benjamin Zephaniah (Puffin)
and one from a double act, *Spill the Beans* is produced by
Paul Cookson and David Harmer (Macmillan Children's
Books).

About Poetry

Michael Rosen's book *'Did I Hear you Write?'* (Five Leaves
Publications) provides a well-argued and, in places,
controversial view of the writing of poetry.
The various contributors to Roger Beard's *Rhyme, Reading
and Writing* (Hodder and Stoughton) explore the
importance of rhyme in the development of children's
reading.

Chapter 6

Performance texts

Playscripts are a text type somewhat underused in primary English. This is partly due to the relatively few scripts written for children. However, they are a dynamic use of language and provide children with a chance not just to read a text but to get up and do it. Texts are not just paper and print. A number of texts are real and used in a performance. The use of a playscript or a joke are examples of texts being read and presented to an audience.

Playscripts

Subject facts

Playscripts have certain distinct features that strike the reader at first glance. Like poetry, playscripts *look* different.

Playscripts are also read in a distinct way – they are read with a view to how they will be performed. The process of the reader using the information on the page to imagine the performance of the play is called transformation. In *An Introduction to Literary Studies* (Routledge), Mario Klarer defined the term transformation as 'the connecting phase between text and performance'.

The information in the script about who says what and who moves where is directed towards a performance of the play on a stage. Of course, when scripts are read in English lessons they are read as texts to be studied. However, to lose sight of that transformation of the text from a playscript into a production is to lose out on so much of what makes reading playscripts a satisfying and dynamic experience.

In reading a playscript the reader encounters three significant features: a setting, dialogue and stage directions.

The setting

A scene in a play will usually open with a description of the setting. For example:

> *Scene: a classroom.*

Scene notes will often include details of the characters who are already on stage. This is an indication of how a scene is created not only by props and background, but also by a set of characters involved in a situation which the audience can connect with. For example:

> *Scene: a bus shelter in front of a derelict house.*

They may even give details as to the mood of the setting:

> *Scene: a bus stop. People are queuing, some with raised umbrellas. It is a miserable day.*

Dialogue

The dialogue makes up the main body of a playscript. This in itself says something about the ways in which we read such texts. The dialogue lines are the words characters say to each other. Unlike stories, there are no passages accompanying the dialogue to explain what a character thinks or feels. Playscripts rely on the reader's transformation of the dialogue to convey much of this information. Lines indicate who says what, for example:

> *Pandora:*   *So what's in the box?*
> *Epimetheus:*   *Don't touch it! Leave it alone!*

But to transform the script, the reader must decide how such lines would be said.

Dialogue conventions

The way characters talk in a playscript, though structured like a conversation between people, is often written in a way that departs from the conventions of everyday speech. Characters don't 'um' and 'ah' in the way people do in natural speech. They don't repeat words as much, don't interrupt or try to interrupt as much and don't use the sorts of fillers that pepper everyday speech. If they did we would have:

Pandora:	So... um... hey? What's in the... the... box... that one...?
Epimetheus:	Don't... er... don't
Pandora:	What...?
Epimetheus:	Don't touch...
Pandora:	But...
Epimetheus:	...it! Leave it alone!

Playscripts often leave out such features, referred to by linguists as normal non-fluency. Part of the transformation of a play may include reinstating such features as part of an attempt to heighten the realistic nature of a production.

Soliloquy

A soliloquy is a long speech, delivered by one character on an empty stage, in which the character reveals his or her true feelings. Through soliloquy a character addresses the audience and expresses his or her feelings, explores a dilemma or explains a situation. In Shakespeare's plays these can present a high level of insight into a character's feelings. In *Hamlet* Act 1 Scene 2, Hamlet's famous soliloquy:

Oh, that this too too solid flesh, would melt...

is preceded by the stage direction:

Exuent all but Hamlet.

At this point, the first time in the play he expresses his feelings, he is the only character on the stage.

Asides

This is the point at which a character addresses the audience directly. The aside is a line said only to the audience, unheard by other characters in the play. For example, in Shakespeare's *Hamlet*:

Hamlet:	...for you yourself, sir, should be old as I am, if, like a crab, you could go backward.
Polonius:	(Aside) *Though this be madness, yet there is a method in't.* Will you walk out of the air, my lord?
Hamlet:	Into my grave?

Here, Polonius gives a quick aside to the audience then continues talking to Hamlet.

Stage directions

Stage direction is the third significant text feature a reader encounters in a playscript. At the start of a scene these are often written in a distinct typeface. They set up the action that is about to follow. During the scene they are often placed in brackets. Stage directions instruct actors what to do and where to go:

> *Pandora enters. She looks bored. She flops into the chair, then sees the box.*

or

> *Pandora:* (picking up the box) *So what's in the box?*

A direction can also indicate an entrance or exit, a gesture or any other movement a character is to make. Stage directions can also indicate a character's emotions as they speak. For example:

> *Pandora:* (inquisitive) *So what's in the box?*

Why you need to know these facts

● Transformation is a vital part of reading a playscript. Scripts are best read with a view towards how they could be transformed into a production. With this in mind, it is worth considering the role children step into as readers of scripts. They are often asked to take parts and, as such, step into the role of actor. However, it is worth asking children to also think of themselves as directors, considering how they would stage the script.

● First and second readings of a playscript have distinctive and important functions. The first reading is a matter of figuring out the storyline, who the characters are and so on. The second reading offers the opportunity to read the scenes and lines with a view to how they contribute to the overall story. This will involve considering what feelings particular characters exhibit in their different scenes and how they relate to one another as the script progresses. Whereas a story can be read once through, it is worth aiming at a second reading of any playscript.

● Playscripts offer an interesting writing form for children to undertake. They are clearly orientated to a specific purpose and audience and focus children's attention on communicating in a different way.

Performance texts

Vocabulary

Aside – a line said directly and only to the audience.
Dialogue – lines characters say to each other.
Soliloquy – a long speech that is spoken only to the audience.
Normal non-fluency – features of speech such as interruption and pausing.
Transformation – interpretation of a playscript into a performance.

Common misconceptions

Performing and drama need to be regarded as separate parts of a school's provision for children. While they will connect at certain points, there is a difference between performance and drama. In the former a script provides the structure for children's acting. In the latter there is the potential for more expressive and exploratory work, as children play out often unscripted scenarios that may not necessarily end up presented to an audience. Performance is always directed by the idea of presentation to an audience.

Teaching ideas

● Script writing is an activity that needs some thought and the children need to be given a manageable task. Children who set out to rewrite the *Star Wars* saga find they have bitten off more than they can chew. Get the children to write scripts for short exchanges such as an argument on the playground.

● Soap operas provide a good stimulus for script writing. As a class, look at the way a soap opera moves around a location such as a village or London square. Decide on a location for a new soap opera and ask the children to devise their own characters and give them the requisite problems. Get them to work in teams of three to script a scene in the life of their character or household. These smaller scripts can be put together to make one episode of the new soap.

● Production notes are a vital part of the transformation of a script. Get the children to annotate copies of a script, noting how particular lines should be said or where characters should move. Remind them that stage directions are not the only emotions or movements made during the acting of a scene. They are just the basics. Tell the children to go back over the script and think of the other emotions and movements needed to transform the script.

● The comedy sketch is a scenario with which older children might be familiar. These tend to be small scripted scenarios centring on an underlying joke or absurdity, such as a cafe that only serves spam. Ask the children to devise their own sketch, starting with a basic comic idea such as a character whose mood swings from pleasant to unpleasant, or a character who does the opposite of what they are told.

● Lines and emotions provide scope for reading shorter sections of playscripts. Ask the children to focus on one short exchange and think carefully about each line. As it is said, what do they think the character is feeling.This works particularly well with sections of Shakespeare.

Wordplay

Subject facts

Like playscripts, wordplay texts are performed for an audience. There are a number of types of text that amuse or entertain their readers or listeners. These range from short texts like calligrams to the lengthy routines of stand-up comedians. The following four examples demonstrate features of such wordplay.

Puns

Puns involve the use of words with similar sounds but different meanings. For example, the old joke:

Question: How do you stay cool in a football match?

Answer: Sit beside a fan.

The joke plays on the double meaning of the word *fan*. Another, older, example can be found Mercutio's dying words in Shakespeare's *Romeo and Juliet*:

Ask for me tomorrow and you shall find me a grave man.

Such jokes usually play with homonyms, words with similar sounds and/or spellings, but different meanings. So the pun on *grave* plays with its two meanings. Some puns play with the different meanings adapted by a word in the question and the answer, for example:

Question: How do you get two whales in a car?

Answer: Drive down the M4.

Calligrams

Calligrams are words represented in a pictorial form. The lettering of the word is produced in a way that represents the meaning of the word, as with the following examples:

Tongue-twisters

Tongue-twisters are sentences that are difficult to say quickly. Classic ones include:

She sells sea shells on the sea shore.

The Leith police dismissed us.

Peter Piper picked a peck of pickled pepper.

Try saying any of these quickly – or even better, three times quickly. The problem with such pieces of wordplay is that they require a quick change between sounds that the mouth makes in different ways. Take the word *picked* from the third example above. To say this quickly the mouth has to move from the *p* sound to the *ck* sound. Making these sounds separately will demonstrate the fact that they are made in completely different ways. But this act of mouth gymnastics is repeated for *peck* and *pickled* – not easy at speed!

Riddles

Riddles involve a question and answer format in which a question is posed followed by an answer that plays with the words used in the question. For example:

Why was the patient's cough better in the morning?

Because he'd been practising all night.

This plays on the meaning of the word *better*, which has the sense of *healed* in the question and *improved upon* in the answer. Many riddles use puns like this, but not all. Some play with the questioner's expectation in the answer:

How do you keep an idiot in suspense?

I'll tell you later.

Some involve something that needs to be figured out in the answer:

What is the difference between a bad marksman and a constipated owl?

A bad marksman shoots but can't hit and a constipated owl...

● Wordplay texts provide a chance for children to work with shorter texts built around a clear idea. As such they give an easy opportunity to compare texts of a similar type and collect a range of examples.

● Wordplay texts are quick to produce – but the process of creating such texts can take ages because of the type of complexity they play with. Puns are not easy to devise, though a list of homonyms provides a starting point that might stimulate writing of such jokes. The shortness of the texts leads to a good opportunity to redraft and refine the writing of such texts.

● Wordplay is an important part of children's language experience. Through such jokes and riddles children acquire an understanding that words can be played with and manipulated, in a way that reinforces their experience of the enjoyment of language.

Why you need to know these facts

Performance texts

Vocabulary

Calligrams – words represented in a pictorial form.
Puns – jokes using words with similar sounds but different meanings.
Riddles – question and answer format in which the answer plays with words used in the question.
Tongue-twisters – sentences that are difficult to say quickly.

Amazing facts

The tongue-twister 'She sells sea shells on the sea shore' was originally a line in a song, made famous by a pantomime comedian, Wilkie Bard, in 1908.

Teaching ideas

● Text collecting is an obvious place to begin work on wordplay. Get the children to sift through school library books for examples of puns or riddles. They can ask at home, ask other staff and gradually produce a collection of the best examples. Stress here should be placed on 'the best'. As was said above, the shortness of these wordplay texts makes them good material with which to explore the editorial task. A riddle collection can involve making judgements about which ones are funniest or have the widest appeal.

● Calligrams make excellent wordplay texts for children to try and produce. Suggest words that may lend themselves to the production of such texts. Items of furniture or household appliances, such as BED or TELEVISION provide a good starting point.

● Tongue-twisters involve a technical construction process. Once they have explored alliteration and assonance (see Chapter 5) children can try putting together a sentence in which two sounds are repeated throughout the line, making the mouth work overtime saying the sentence. Examples from children include (try saying each of them three times, quickly!):

Dean nodded in a dinner ladies dinner.

Take ten cats to a cat cart track.

Performance Plays (Scholastic)
This series of playscripts provides a range of stories in dramatised form aimed at different age ranges. The scripts include directions and indications as to how lines should be said. There are also workshop sessions for working with children on the script and production notes giving guidance on staging, scenery and rehearsal. Plays include:

For 5–7 year olds:
Peter's Problem
The Clown who couldn't Smile
The War of the Vegetables

For 7–9 year olds:
A Suitably Happy Ending
Crime Doesn't Pay

For 8–10 year olds:
The Pied Piper of Hamelin
Three Murders, a Suicide and a Near Miss

For 9–11 year olds:
Hamlet, the Murder Mystery
Love Me Tender
The Big Ship Sails

Language Play, by David Crystal (Penguin)
An entertaining guide to some of the various ways in which writers, puzzle specialists and comedians, among others, play with words.

Chapter 7
Media texts

In recent years schools have increasingly developed an awareness of the importance of media education and media studies is now available as an examination course in a number of secondary schools. In primary schools there has been a gradual move towards considering media texts, such as soap operas, comics, cartoons, films and videos, critically. This chapter will focus on the two types of media texts that are commonly used in the teaching of literacy: newspapers and advertising. However, it is worth acknowledging at the outset that these are only the tip of the media iceberg and there is much more that merits exploration in this field.

Adverts

Subject facts

The word advert stems from the Latin words *ad* meaning 'to' and *vertere* meaning 'turn'. The purpose of such texts is to turn readers towards something. In her useful guide to advertising, *The Language of Advertising* (Routledge), Angela Goddard builds on this definition by pointing out that an advert is produced with the conscious intention of benefiting the originator, either through increasing sales of a product or participation in some activity.

In this chapter we will limit our overview of advertising

to printed texts and how they use the words and images to appeal to their audience.

Image

Poster hoardings, full page adverts in magazines and posters in shops and cinemas are the sorts of adverts that bring home the significance of images in advertising. Cinema and video posters, such as the advert for *Chicken Run* below, are often dominated by one large image.

© 2000 Dreamworks, Pathe and Aardman

From this image we might gather that *Chicken Run* will be a spoof adventure film – with the heroines being chickens and the villain being rather gormless.

Layout

The balance between the words and images and the arrangement of these features on the page is worth looking at in advertising. In a film poster there will often be large, clear wording that catches the reader's eye, intrigues them and suggests what genre the film is. For example, 'A saga is born...' or 'Are you ready for a scare?' The caption 'This ain't no chick flick', suggests the film is a comedy.

Smaller print will carry other information, such as the name of the scriptwriter and composer of the film score. It can be interesting to look at the font size of the various items of text included on an advert. Above, the third largest piece of text tells us that *Chicken Run* is from the team who created 'Wallace and Gromit'.

Product name

Adverts will usually include the name of the product being advertised. The branding of a product is an important part of consumer appeal. A number of these brand names go through a long process of consideration.

Slogans

Slogans are short sentences or phrases attached to a particular product. A number of products are marketed through the use of slogans that feature throughout a range of adverts in an advertising campaign. Consider 'The bank that likes to say "Yes"' or 'The listening bank', both of which were used repeatedly till they became fixed in people's minds. Age-old slogans such as 'Beans Meanz Heinz' or 'Go to work on an egg' became part of popular culture.

Advertising copy

Advertising copy is the text that makes up the advert. Along with the textual features mentioned above, adverts may also include a body of text that makes claims about the product or explains how it works. Such language will often use wordplay to draw the reader's attention. For example, one advert for Chrysler shows a luxury helicopter on the left of the advert and Chrysler car on the right with the caption: 'How the discerning American gets around. And a helicopter.' This leaves the reader to pick apart the relationship between picture and caption. The longer this takes, the longer the reader's attention is being captivated by the advert.

The British Airways advert below is an example of such language play at work, asking the reader to figure out what is missing.

In *The Cambridge Encyclopedia of the English Language*, David Crystal states that the wording used in such text:

> *...tends to use words which are vivid* (new, bright), *concrete* (soft, washable), *positive* (safe, extra), *and unreserved* (best, perfect).

This succinct analysis of the language of advertising could be used as a checklist for considering the claims that feature in a range of adverts. For example, consider the following advert for Marks and Spencer's peaches:

> *All our peaches are individually chosen. They're handpicked from the sunniest outside branches. So they're plumper, sweeter and juicier. For the freshest fruit pick Sunburst at Marks & Spencer.*

Here we have:

> *vivid:* sunniest... branches
> *concrete:* plumper
> *positive:* sweeter and juicier
> *unreserved:* for the freshest...

Appeal to the audience

Stepping back from the various facets of advertising, it is worth returning to Goddard's point about advertising involving personal gain. Two vital features of an advert's selling power are the claims made for the product and the appeal made to the audience.

Claims involve presenting the product in the sort of language Crystal described above. An advert will present a product's unique selling points. Sometimes referred to in jargon as USPs (<u>u</u>nique <u>s</u>elling <u>p</u>oints) these are the specific things a product has that outmatch what is on offer from rival competitors.

Adverts will often use comparative language, but they will use it with care. They don't make direct comparison, for example 'Our peaches are plumper than the ones in Saleprice'. However, as Angela Goddard points out:

> *Their lack of specific reference to other products doesn't stop advertisers from employing comparative reference... what they do is leave out the comparative item.*

So the Marks and Spencer's advert quoted above uses adjectives like *juicier* and *sweeter* without saying 'juicier than X's peaches'.

Adverts have a target audience at which they are aimed. The Chrysler advert quoted above constructed an image of the 'discerning American' and, in doing so, presented a type of person to the audience. The advert is appealing to readers to identify themselves with that sort of person and, as a result, want to drive their type of car.

Some adverts target their audience by presenting a problem or need with which the audience will identify. The NSPCC advert quoted below prompted its audience to think about the long-term effects of child poverty and abuse.

Why you need to know these facts

● Advertising texts are everywhere, in magazines and comics, in newspapers, on posters, at sporting venues and so on. The prevalence of such texts means they are visible to children from a very young age. A number of anecdotes about children learning to read relate the way in which children learned distinctive logos for products at a young age. As such, adverts make interesting texts to bring into the classroom. When we use adverts we draw on an aspect of popular culture that children are sure to encounter in their daily lives.

● Critical awareness is a vital part of the teaching of literacy, particularly where adverts are concerned. By involving children in picking apart and creating their own adverts they can be shown the sort of techniques adverts use to appeal to their audience. This can make them more able to critically evaluate the claims of adverts.

● Adverts tend to be short texts. As such they provide a good resource for rereading and careful consideration. Having analysed the claims of one advert, children soon become able to critically evaluate the claims of another.

● Adverts provide a good field in which children can develop their critical skills. It may be something of a reflection of teacher attitudes but children are more likely to be negatively critical about adverts. They are more likely to disagree with them, find fault in them and question the claims they make.

● Adverts provide one of the most accessible ways for children to appreciate the various ways in which media texts vary on regular printed text. The typographic differences and use of a picture are just the start of the particular nature of these texts. There is also the way in which such texts can feature puzzles or games for the reader, such as the British Airways advert on page 142.

such as the British Airways advert on page 142.

Vocabulary

Advert – a text that markets or sells something.
Copy – text of an advert or news story.
Slogans – short sentences or phrases attached to a particular product.
Typographic differences – the differences in the way text is presented, for example the font sizes and types.
USP – the unique selling point of a product, making it more marketable than rivals.

Common misconceptions

The images and words in adverts don't always match neatly. When looking at the text and image of an advert it is worth noticing the way in which adverts can make use of a contrast between the two. The text says one thing, the picture says another and the reader is left looking longer at the advert thinking it through.

A powerful series of adverts issued by the NSPCC did just this. One showed the image of a baby in an alleyway with drugs – the caption read 'John Donaldson, Age 23'. Another showed a young boy about to jump off a roof, accompanied by the wording, 'Martin Ward, Age 29'. The adverts went on to explain the link between the childhood problems of these two people that led them to 'a hopeless future'.

Amazing facts

Angela Goddard illustrates the way in which the language used in advertising does not always translate easily between languages. She explains that the Pepsi slogan:

Come alive with the Pepsi generation.

was translated into Chinese as:

Pepsi will bring your ancestors back from the dead.

Kentucky Fried Chicken's:

Finger lickin' good.

was translated as:

Eat your finger off.

● Start by asking the children to collect or write down slogans they already know. As well asking them to remember written texts, ask them to relate slogans they remember from television adverts. Create a class collection of slogans on a large chart on the classroom wall. Ask the children to look at the brevity of the slogans and the use of rhyme or wordplay. Ask them to try constructing their own slogans to advertise an imaginary product or the name of their school.

● Advert grids provide a chance for children to compare a range of adverts. The grid involves a range of questions about adverts along the column headings:
– *Product.* What is the name and type of product (for example, Mondeo, a car)?
– *Target audience.* Who is the advert targeting? How old are these people? What sorts of things do they like?
– *Claims about the product.* What is the most affirmative language used about the product?
– *Adjectives.* What are the particularly interesting uses of descriptive language?
– *Image used.* What pictures are featured in the advert?
   Ask the children to collect and compare a range of adverts for similar products such as cars, sweets or computers. Tell them to use the grid to analyse their adverts. This can sometimes bring out similar claims or images between adverts.

● Devising adverts is a good way of pooling the knowledge gained from looking at a range of examples. Without the grounding in examples, it is an activity that falls a bit flat, but, building on the details picked out in this section, ask the children to construct adverts. Tell them to follow the pattern of language, to use a carefully chosen image and to target a particular audience. They could also work in groups and devise a series of adverts to comprise a campaign.

● Advertising can provide scope for a productive investigation into where and how the text type is used. To fill out the class's perspective on the way advertising works, as a class investigate the various groups involved in making and regulating adverts. Contact manufacturers or agencies to ask for samples of ad campaigns; contact the press to find out the cost of advertising space; or find out about the role of the Advertising Standards Authority.

Newspaper reading is a deeply individualised practice.
There are those of us who read the headlines and photo
captions in a tabloid, others who begin at the sports pages
and work forwards. Some will turn straight to a favourite
columnist, others to the cartoons. What is clear from
looking at the ways in which newspaper readers handle
their texts is that there are certain common features of
newspapers that readers use to instinctively guide their
reading.

Subject facts

The example here shows a front page from The Mirror. It
exhibits some of the common features that can be found in
news stories:

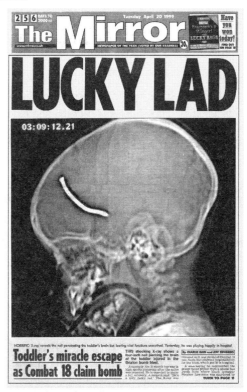

The headline
The headline is short and clear. It catches the reader's
attention and gives some idea of the content of the story. In
this case the use of the headline 'Lucky Lad' indicates the

story is about a child, prompting a level of human interest. The headline is devised after the story has been written.

A standfirst

A standfirst is a short sentence that fills out some detail of the story. It is in a smaller font than the headline but larger than the story. In this case two aspects of the story are highlighted for the reader in the standfirst: 'Toddler's miracle escape as Combat 18 claim bomb'. Firstly the fact that this was a very young child whose escape was miraculous and secondly that the perpetrators of the vicious attack were Combat 18. Standfirsts join with headlines to draw readers further into a story.

A byline

A byline gives the name of the reporter or the story. The byline for the article 'Lucky Lad' here is 'By Charlie Bain and Jeff Edwards'. Sometimes a byline will include the reporter's specialism, for example 'by Harry Harris, Chief Football Writer'.

The image

Some stories will include a picture usually accompanied by a caption. In the case of the 'Lucky Lad' story the picture presents the X-ray of the child showing the damage and narrow escape at the hands of a nail bomb. The caption read:

> HORRIFIC: X-ray reveals the nail penetrating the toddler's brain but leaving vital functions unscathed. Yesterday he was playing happily in hospital.

The masthead

Given that this is a front page to the paper it also includes the common front page masthead giving the paper's title, *The Mirror*.

Copy

Copy is, as in advertising, the content of the article. It is the text that makes up the story. The first paragraph often communicates much of the general information of the story, aiming to answer the main questions about the item: who, what, when, where and why. This is done in one clear sentence. For example, coverage of a celebrity's plane crash in 1999 opened with:

Broadcaster Peter Snow told yesterday how he cheated death when the plane he was on crashed into a forest.
Rosa Prince, *The Mirror*, 4th October 1999

This gives us, in one sentence:

Broadcaster Peter Snow (who) *told yesterday* (when) *how he cheated death* (what) *when the plane he was on crashed* (why) *into a forest* (where).

Stories vie for space in a newspaper and journalists have to clearly communicate information within a limited number of words. The language isn't flowery, description is kept to a minimum and the story must be accurate. In *Journalism for Beginners* (Piatkus), Joan Clayton gives the rule 'WORDS MUST WORK', and points out that adjectives are often unnecessary and journalists must avoid repetition, obscurity and opinion. She goes on to say:

Use the least number of words possible – EVERY WORD MUST BE NECESSARY. It must have a job to do or it shouldn't be there.

The audience
As with advertising, newspapers are constructed with an understanding of the audience they will reach. Comparing the amount of space given to the same story in different papers and the stories that find a place on a paper's front page can give a clear indication of this agenda at work. A hurricane can strike an Asian city on the same day a pop star marries a footballer. Different papers will give different levels of prominence to each story. One influencing factor at work here is McLurg's law. McLurg, the editor who formulated the rule, pointed out that the reader's interest in a story grew less and less in accordance with their distance from it (see Carol Craggs, *Media Education in the Primary School*, Routledge).

● A newspaper provides an effective structure for teaching. While a caption may seem obvious to those of us who are familiar with newspapers, to a child flicking through a tabloid and captivated by a particular image the caption is an essential to understanding the link between the pictures and the story. Similarly the sort of instinctive skimming (see Chapter 3, page 72) of newspapers is rooted in an awareness of the conventions that underpin opening paragraphs.

Why you need to know these facts

Media texts

● Children can begin to read news stories from a very young age. (As someone who started reading *The Daily Mirror* at the age of five, I can recommend early access to newspaper stories.) Children of reception age can look at items of news, particularly those accompanied by a stark and interesting picture and can begin to ask questions about the news items. They can also follow the way in which an adult answers these questions by locating information in the text.

● Awareness of the features of news reporting can enhance the accessibility of the text to young readers. Like any text, news reporting has its own conventions. A feature like the standfirst can become something children look out for as a way of making such texts more readable.

● Critical appreciation of news reporting stems from the need for readers to evaluate what they read. Stories in the news will prompt opinion but there is also a need for children to be aware that such stories are not just facts dropping from the sky – they are put together by a writer who made conscious choices in the production of the text. Looking at why a reporter used a particular standfirst or quoted a particular participant in events is a part of such critical reading. Children also need to be aware of the distinction between fact and opinion, looking out for where stories explain the facts of an event and the opinions of those involved.

Vocabulary

Byline – the name of a reporter on a news story.
Headline – large title of a news story.
Masthead – newspaper's title.
Standfirst – a short sentence that fills out some detail of the story.

Amazing facts

In *Media Education in the Primary School* (Routledge), Carol Craggs gives an insight into why the first paragraph needs to carry so much of a news story's factual content:

> *Space is always tight – there are so many pieces to cram on each page. In the frantic rush of production, stories are cut [from the end] without being read… But the editor knows, without having to read it, that because the piece is written to the formula, the full story is there [in the first paragraph].*

● Writing news stories is, like advertising, an activity that needs to be supported by some idea of the conventions that can be seen in such texts. Trimming words to the bare essentials, removing opinion, producing standfirsts, headlines and a clear opening paragraph will give structure to children's news reporting. It can also provide an alternative way of gathering the children's own news, relating facts and quotes from events in which they were involved and thinking up a headline for the story. Alternatively they can compile items of school news, interviewing staff and parents for comment.

● Headlines can provide scope for initial work on newspapers. Get the children to sum up a current news story or a personal story in a catchy headline. Alternatively they could imagine they are reporting on a fairy story and come up with their own headline for it. For example:

Puss boots giant.

Mystery woman gives Prince the slipper.

● Give the children a set of headlines and ask them to hazard ideas about the story that could follow them. Following a headline like 'Lucky Lad' they may gather what kind of person is involved (a lad – suggesting a young boy), whereas 'Lucky I'm alive' gives some idea that someone could have died. Give the children copies of actual stories, separated from their headlines, and ask them to match each story to its headline.

● Reading news stories is an activity open to some variety. Ask the children to bring in a favourite story from a week of news reporting. When doing this sort of activity it is worth having a set of current papers in class for use by those who don't have access to a paper at home. However, the homework aspect can provide some discussion and prompting of thoughts and opinions from home.

You could also, as a class, read one news story in a range of different papers. This will give insight into the different ways papers handle news items. They can begin to see more sensational aspects of reporting and begin to decide which type of reporting they prefer.

Another variation is to track an ongoing story over a period of weeks. This can involve following how a story breaks over a period of days and weeks.

● Local papers are well worth contacting when doing work on news. Some provide pages for children to contribute news stories to, others will send out a reporter to meet children and talk to them. A visit can be an interesting chance to see a massive printing press rolling away. It can also result in a report on the children's interest featuring in the next edition of the paper.

Resources

Advertising
The Language of Advertising, by Angela Goddard (Routledge)
This entertaining guide to advertising manages to complement a clear analysis of some of the main features of this text type with interesting reflections on the world of advertising.

Newspapers
Journalism for Beginners, by Joan Clayton (Piatkus)
Written for prospective journalists, this book also conveys some clear information about news reporting, giving particularly interesting insights into the style of journalistic writing.

Media
Media Education in the Primary School, by Carol Craggs (Routledge)
This excellent title includes material on some of the more visual aspects of media literacy not covered in this chapter.

Understanding texts
Glossary

Advertisement – a text that markets or sells something.
Alliteration – the repetition of a consonant sound.
Annotating – making marks on a text.
Aside – a line said directly and only to the audience.
Assonance – the repetition of a vowel sound.
Binary key – a chart that subdivides categories using a tree structure in which categories branch into sub-categories.
Byline – the name of a reporter on a news story.
Calligrams – words represented in a pictorial form.
Causal connectives – connecting words and phrases that show how one thing caused or was caused by another thing.
Causality – the effect of one thing causing another.
Characterisation – the process by which a story builds up a picture of a character.
Chorus – repeated lines between the verses of a song or poem.
Chronological order – the order in which events occur in time.
Cinquain – a poem consisting of five lines with the syllable structure two–four–six–eight–two.
Clerihew – a short summation of a person in two rhyming couplets.
Cohesion – the links across a text, one sentence linking with another.
Copy – text of an advert or news story.
Couplets – two rhyming lines next to each other.
Covert narration – narration where the narrative voice is not obvious.
Dialogue – the lines that characters say to each other.
Direct characterisation – direct presentation of information about a character in a text.

Dialect – a distinctive variety of grammar and vocabulary, often connected to a particular region.

Discussion texts – texts that explore the various positions that can be taken up on an issue.

Explanation texts – texts that outline a process, explaining how or why something happens.

Field – the content and purpose of an act of communication.

First person narration – the telling of a story in the voice of one of the main characters in the story, for example 'I saw Natalie and we went shopping'.

Flashbacks – a point at which a story 'flashes back' to events that took place earlier.

Free verse – poetry free from restrictions of rhyme and metre.

Generalised events – events that happen again and again (for example, rockets taking off) rather than at one particular moment in history (such as Apollo 10 taking off).

Generalised participants – general categories such as 'the frog' rather than specific characters such as 'Kermit the Frog'.

Genre – a grouping of similar texts.

Glossary – a section of a non-fiction text that lists and defines technical or specialist terminology.

Haiku – a poem consisting of three lines with the syllable structure five–seven–five.

Headline – large title of a news story.

Hints – small pieces of information or advice within an instruction text.

Imperative verbs – words that command the reader to do something, for example *boil a kettle, cut the paper*.

Indirect characterisation – the use of diverse features such as the actions or speech to build up an overall picture of a character.

Instruction texts – texts outlining a set of steps towards a particular goal.

Language feature – particular aspects of the language of texts, such as common verb tenses or particular types of word usage.

Masthead – newspaper's title.

Metre – the rhythm created by the syllable structure of lines of poetry.

Modal verbs – verbs that express the likelihood or certainty of other verbs. If, for example, someone says 'I make boats' then there is no doubting the statement. Modal verbs, such as *could* or *will* express how certain an action is, for example 'I *could* make boats', 'I *will* make boats'.

Mode – the means of communication, such as a letter.

Mood – atmosphere or feeling conjured up in a story.

Narrative poetry – a storyline told in a poem.

Narrative privilege – the way in which the narrative voice can relate things a pure observer would not have seen, such as how a particular character was feeling.

Narrator – the voice that 'tells' a story.

Non-chronological – not structured according to the passage of time.

Normal non-fluency – features of speech such as interruption and pausing.

Orientation – an opening section of a text giving some idea of the events to be presented in a recount.

Overt narration – times when the narrative voice becomes more obvious.

Past tense – verb forms for events that have taken place, for example *ran, walked.*

Pentameter – a line of poetry with five metrical feet.

Persuasive texts – texts that aim to influence the reader towards a particular opinion.

Phonetics – the sounds of human speech.

Plot – that which connects the events in a story, with one event causing another.

Point of view – the presentation of events from the viewpoint of a particular character.

Prediction – anticipation of what might take place at a later stage in a story.

Prepositions – words that indicated where or when something is in relation to something else, for example *under, on, before.*

Procedural texts – a term sometimes used for instruction texts.

Puns – jokes using words with similar sounds but different meanings.

Rap – poetry from within the reggae tradition of Jamaica with a strong rhythm.

Recount – a text that records a series of events.

Register – conventions that underpin certain uses of language.

Report texts – texts that present information on a subject, creating 'a picture in words'.

Rhyme – the effect created when the endings of words sound alike, for example *cat/hat.*

Roles – different parts characters play in the events of a story.

Route diagram – a chart that connects various pieces of information in a sequence.

Scanning – the location of particular words or features within a text.

Setting – the location, place or time, in which a story is set.
Simple present tense – the simple present form of a verb, for example *make, find*.
Skimming – quick 'reading' of a text to locate main features, content and structure.
Slogans – short sentences or phrases attached to a particular product.
Soliloquy – a long speech that is spoken only to the audience.
Spidergram – a chart that elaborates the various pieces of information stemming from a subject.
Standfirst – a short sentence that fills out some detail of the story.
Storylines – a series of events organised into a story.
Structure – how a text is organised; the relationship of the parts of a text.
Sub-headings – headings used to subdivide information in a non-fiction text.
Synthesising – the organising of a set of facts in a systematic way.
Tenor – relationship between participants in an act of communication, for example teacher–child, bank manager–customer.
Tetrameter – a line of poetry with four metrical feet.
Theme – important ideas or issues in a text.
Third person narration – story told in the voice of someone removed from the events, for example 'He saw Natalie and they went shopping'.
Temporal connectives – connecting words that link things in time, for example *then*, *later*, and *after this*.
'Timeless' present tense – the present tense of the verb, as in what the subject does at present, for example 'the caterpillar *lives*, it *breathes*'.
Tongue-twisters – sentences that are difficult to say quickly.
Traits – features of characters.
Transformation – interpretation of a playscript into a performance.
Typography – the print or 'type' style on a page, such as bold or italic lettering or the font used.
Unreliable narrator – a narrator whose record of events is unreliable – possibly due to opinion or bias.
USP – the unique selling point of a product, making it more marketable than rivals.
Verse – a group of lines forming a section of a poem.

Understanding texts

Index